Secret Recipe

Secret Recipe

Why KFC is Still Cookin' after 50 Years

by Robert Darden

Tapestry Press
Irving, Texas

Tapestry Press
3649 Conflans Road
Suite 103
Irving, TX 75061

Printed in the United States of America

08 07 06 05 04   5 4 3 2 1

Library of Congress Cataloging-in-Publication Data on request

Darden, Bob, 1954-
    Secret recipe : why KFC is still cookin' after 50 years / by Robert
Darden.
        p. cm.
Includes index.
    ISBN 1-930819-12-9 (acid-free paper)
    ISBN 1-930819-33-1 (trade paper cover, acid-free paper)
    1. Kentucky Fried Chicken (Firm) 2. Restaurant management. I. Title.
TX945.5.K46 D37 2002
338.7'616479573—dc21

                         2002000340

Book design and layout by D. & F. Scott Publishing,
N. Richland Hills, Texas

To
Matthew Grayson, Sydney Darden,
Wynne Darden and Daniel Mayfield:

Treat every meal as if it were communion.
Treat every job as the most important one in the world.
Treat every person the way
you would want to be treated.

Pete Harman

Contents

Acknowledgments

Thanks to everyone who opened their homes, their scrapbooks, and their memories to me while assembling material for this book.

Special thanks to Michele Sheridan, Rick Weber, Nelle Zeydel, and Jeff Lightburn for making the KFC and Harman archives available to me, for scheduling interviews with KFC greats, past and present, and for never once saying, "Umm, we'd prefer that you *not* use that."

I also would like to acknowledge the contributions of three books published about Colonel Harland Sanders: his autobiography, *Life As I Have Known It Has Been Finger Lickin' Good*; *The Colonel: The Captivating Biography of the Dynamic Founder of a Fast-Food Empire* by John Ed Pearce; and *The Colonel's Secret: Eleven Herbs and a Spicy Daughter* by Margaret Sanders.

Robert Darden
Fall 2001

Introduction
What's in the Secret Recipe?

"The Colonel was my teacher and a pacesetter for the industry. He was the most exciting man I have ever known. He was a motivator, and he was one of those most responsible for emphasizing quality in the restaurant business. He wanted the customer to have the best and didn't care how hard it was to achieve that."
—Dave Thomas, founder of Wendy's Restaurants

The title *Secret Recipe* may suggest that I've uncovered the highly guarded secret ingredients to KFC's food. I wish I had, but the folks at KFC can rest easy—the secret recipe remains secret.

But I have discovered something that I consider equally important: insight into what has enabled KFC to become an enduring and successful American icon for fifty years. While the food is certainly the hero, I believe that the true reason for the phenomenal success of KFC is the values of the people who shaped that corporation.

The end result is that this is a book within a book—a tale of two unassuming men who shaped a business that would affect the lives of hundreds of thousands of people the world over. Their pervasive influence has meant that virtually every KFC franchisee has looked to them for support and guidance.

Secret Recipe is the story of how Colonel Harland Sanders brought his dream and vision alive, and lived to see it become an international success. Equally important, it's a story about Leon "Pete" Harman, who became much more than KFC's first and largest franchisee. He became a leader of not only his own individual franchise but also of KFC at large.

Together, the Colonel and Harman forged a bond that changed each of their lives *and* the future of dining throughout the world.

At first glance, Pete Harman and Colonel Sanders made an unlikely pair: Pete, the quiet family man, the soft-spoken Mormon, the gifted businessman; the Colonel, brash and outspoken, a showman, a genius in the kitchen. But they complemented each other.

More than fate brought the two together in 1952. The Colonel had perfected the method to make "the best damn fried chicken you've ever put in your mouth." He also had the idea to franchise his innovation long before the American business community made it a common practice.

Pete Harman then brought the Colonel's idea to life in his own restaurant and named the concept "Kentucky Fried Chicken." Other innovations over the years—from introducing the "bucket" to creating employee-ownership programs and putting women in key management positions—came from Harman as well and were quickly adopted by KFC.

The story of the Kentucky Fried Chicken phenomenon, however, is more than mere biography. It is the story of a billion Sunday dinners served every day of the week. It is about a regional dish that has become a worldwide dining treat, a symbol of American mystique right up there with the Model T Ford and *The Wizard of Oz*.

KFC's history is also about the birth of the suburb, the dominance of the automobile, the emergence of women in the permanent workforce, and the rise of the quick-service food industry.

From the beginning, before the white suit and the goatee, Harland Sanders was obsessed with excellence. He believed that his was the best chicken in the world and that if people anywhere would just try it, they would agree. When the Colonel visited a KFC restaurant, he didn't stand in the dining room gabbing with the owner. He made a beeline to the kitchen, where he sampled gravy and ran his gloved fingers over doorjambs looking for dust.

 *Introduction*

When Pete Harman needed vice presidents to operate his constantly expanding operation, he didn't bring in MBAs in navy blue suits from East Coast universities. He hired long-time waitresses and cooks who knew how to please customers and fry chicken until it was *just so*.

Throughout my interviews and sessions with the people of KFC, the same message rang out time and time again—these two icons spent a lifetime taking care of the people who worked with them, and those people in turn did whatever it took to please their customers.

That is the basis for *Secret Recipe*. And these are the lessons I've learned—eleven ingredients for business success. It seems to me that they are universal and timeless for *any* business, applicable to everything from fried chicken to automobiles to stocks and bonds.

KFC's Secret Recipe

1. Honesty and hard work pay off.

All of the following principles are equally important, but this is perhaps the moral to the story, and the final enduring value Colonel Sanders and Pete Harman leave for future generations. By virtue of their own life experiences and accomplishments, this "golden rule" inspires everyone across the KFC system to achieve his or her own personal best.

2. Always give back to your community.

KFC and Pete Harman have always shared their success with others and have consistenly reinvested in the communities where they do business. KFC is truly a part of every hometown.

3. Franchisees bring a special passion and commitment to growing your business.

This has been the lifeblood for KFC—even in the toughest of times. The system has one of the most loyal and seasoned groups of franchise owners in any industry. Together, they offer

tremendous experience and ideas, and they invest in the business by opening new units. This is a strong competitive weapon.

4. Success is in the details—every penny counts.

Running a restaurant means doing a thousand things well every day and every hour, and successful KFC restaurant managers know their business inside and out. They know how to make their customers happy and how to make a buck at the same time.

5. Make employees owners in your business and they'll think and act like owners.

Pete Harman and KFC find ways to make people owners in the business. People no longer think of themselves as merely paid employees; instead, they have a stake in the business. This unleashes tremendous potential and energy.

6. Serve up food that's so good it brings customers back.

It's always been about the food and its unique flavors—serving it hot and fresh to every customer each and every time they visit KFC. This gives people a reason to return, and it helps build sales.

7. If you lose quality, you lose it all.

This is a hard lesson, learned by KFC over the years whenever it strayed from its core competency. But every time KFC renewed its emphasis on food quality (something they call "Re-Colonelization"), customers returned in droves.

8. Run each restaurant like it's your only one.

In the beginning, it was simpler to run a handful of excellent restaurants. KFC today prides itself on avoiding the "averages" by striving for excellence in operating thousands of restaurants globally.

9. *The customer's opinion is what counts.*

Pete Harman and the Colonel relentlessly drove this value far and deep, emphasizing the need to constantly listen and respond to your customers—and doing whatever it takes to make them happy.

10. *Have a point of difference—and drive it.*

KFC begins by differentiating itself with its food. But it's also much more, as everything it does—from its advertising and promotions to building design and layout—sets it apart and sends a clear signal to customers.

11. *Recognition is a powerful way to attract and keep good people.*

Pete Harman wrote the book on how to motivate people through genuine, heartfelt recognition. Today, KFC recognizes its employees in many ways, but the most powerful is the individual and personal recognition people give to one another.

These eleven ingredients are not displayed on a plaque anywhere, they are not in a dry-as-dust Human Resources manual, yet they are practiced daily. These ingredients are certainly not new to the world of business—they are simply good common sense.

But the secret is this—together, they are powerful, life-changing mandates that can transform companies as surely as they can transform individual lives.

Robert Darden
Fall 2001

On the Colonel's 82nd birthday, the state of Kentucky erected a historical marker at the site of the original Sanders restaurant in Corbin, Kentucky.

The Colonel, an American Icon

Perhaps it takes a difficult and demanding life to produce something that endures. Harland David Sanders had such a life. His twin defining characteristics—a passion for excellence and a dogged persistence—were shaped by that hardscrabble life. And that life was instrumental in forging an international brand that has prospered beyond Harland Sanders' wildest dreams.

The secrets that a life of deprivation and constant adversity taught young Harland were both hard-won and universal. Raised in the direst poverty, he resolved at an impossibly early age to do more than survive—he vowed to succeed. And success did come, through the sheer force of his will and a simple formula:

Honesty and hard work pay off.

Every time.

From a practical standpoint, the secret of his early success may be found in a simple promise printed at the top of his first menu:

"Howdy folks, I promise you a good meal. If it's not, don't pay for it."

—Harland Sanders

Two decades after his death, Col. Harland Sanders remains an iconographic figure in American popular culture. He's as recognizable as Mickey Mouse, Betty Crocker, Tony the Tiger, and Uncle Sam. Yet he alone of that list was a real person. "The Colonel," as he was universally called, was a complicated, sometimes contradictory man. He was both revered and feared. He was rough-edged and charming. He had a sixth-grade education and he had a world of street smarts. He was deeply religious and he was frequently profane. And few childhoods were less auspicious . . .

Where It All Began

Harland David Sanders was born on September 9, 1890, outside the small town of Henryville in southern Indiana, the eldest of three children of Wilburt and Margaret Dunlevy Sanders. His father, a farmer and sometime butcher, died when Harland was only five, leaving his mother to sharecrop an eighty-acre farm.

Sanders told *The New Yorker* in 1970 that while his mother was away working, he watched over his siblings, foraged for sassafras buds and May apples by day, and went to bed on his own at night. He also developed a fiercely independent spirit.

> *"We didn't have any babysitter, but we got along fine. We knowed enough not to burn the house down—I don't know why kids are so different today."*
> —Harland Sanders

Sanders often said that by carefully watching his mother in the kitchen, he eventually excelled in cooking, especially vegetables. He baked his first loaf of bread from scratch at the age of seven and took it to the tomato-canning factory in Henryville three miles away to show his mother who worked there. Thus began a lifelong love affair with food.

In later years, Sanders would point to a second incident as being one of the turning points in his life, one that helped define who he was until his final days. At age ten, Sanders was hired by a local farmer to clear some land for two dollars a month plus room and board. But, as Sanders often told the story, the young boy simply enjoyed wandering about the uncut wilderness. The job was secondary.

"I sure liked it out there. Squirrels was runnin' up and down the trees. Butterflies and redbirds was flitterin' from sassafras and witch hazel bushes to dogwood and black gum trees. Maybe I watched them more than I should of. So by the end of the first month, I cleared only about an acre of ground."

The farmer was furious:

"One whole month and that's all you got done? Boy, you ain't worth a daggone. I ain't gonna feed you for that. You go on home! I don't need you no more."

Young Harland trudged home, fighting back tears, fully expecting a serious scolding. "She was a-sittin' at the big table in the kitchen readin' the Bible. She looked tired, I thought, and I sure hated to tell her the news about my bein' fired off my job.

"'Son,' she asked, 'why are you home?'

"'Mr. Norris didn't like the work I'd done, so he let me go,' I told it truthful.

"'It looks like you'll never amount to anything. I'm afraid you're just no good. Here I am, left alone with you three children to support, and you're my oldest boy, the only one that can help me, and you won't even work enough so somebody will keep you. I guess I'll never be able to count on you.'

"By the time she got through her tongue-lashing, I felt just about as low as a snake's belly. I felt so remorseful to think I had let my mom down like I did.

"I made a resolve right then and there: If I ever get a job again, nothing will ever keep me from finishin' what I'm called on to do."

3

Sanders' mother remarried a few years later, and the family moved to Greenwood, Indiana. But it quickly became apparent that he did not get along with his stepfather, a moody, taciturn truck farmer.

At age twelve, Sanders left home and school on the same day, no longer able to tolerate his abusive stepfather. He took with him a cardboard suitcase and an explosive temper that would follow him the rest of his life. Sanders bounced from job to job before illegally enlisting in the army at age sixteen in 1906. The army shipped him out to Cuba on a transport carrier with 1,500 mules. Buffeted by the churning sea and sickened by the smell of mule manure, Sanders quickly lost his desire for army life and was discharged four months later at his request.

Back in the United States, he tried a variety of jobs before ending up in Jasper, Alabama, working on the railroad. Here he met his first wife, Josephine King, at the local movie house. As Sanders recalled it, he was bashful and tongue-tied around girls. After a shy courtship, they were married in 1910. Several years later, after he lost his job, Josephine left him, taking their children—Margaret, Mildred, and Harland Jr.—with her and moving back home with her parents. The couple later reconciled, but Sanders wrote that the marriage never recovered.

Always an avid reader despite his lack of education, Harland eventually practiced law in the Justice of the Peace Court in Little Rock, Arkansas, where no law degree was required. The fledgling law practice and hours spent arguing legal matters produced an unexpected talent, that of an actor. He developed an uncanny ability to portray any character that would give him an edge in the courtroom. And he found that he loved the attention. He basked in the limelight.

When the Arkansas state legislature abolished Sanders' position, he was "on the road" again, taking on a dizzying array of jobs. After yet another stint with the railroads, Harland sold insurance, sold stock in a ferry company, joined Rotary International, manufactured an acetylene lighting system, sold insurance again, and sold a lot of Michelin tires in Kentucky.

Sanders told his daughters that he always felt "called" to Kentucky, that he wanted to do something to improve life in the mountain region of his beloved chosen state. According to his daughter Margaret, he was "haunted by the sheer devastation of life in the mountains."

At age thirty-four, Sanders was thriving as a tire salesman, but found himself unemployed once again when Michelin closed its New Jersey plant. Then a chance encounter with the general manager of the Standard Oil Company of Kentucky led to ownership of a service station in Nicholasville, twelve miles from Lexington.

As a traveling tire salesman, Sanders had bypassed other gas stations to fill up at one particular establishment where the owners checked his oil and tire pressure, cleaned his windows, and whisked his seats. He operated his station the same way. He opened at 5:00 AM (two hours before his competitors) and stayed late in the night patching flats. Soon he was selling up to 1,800 gallons of gas a month—more than any other station in northern Kentucky.

But the stock market crash of 1929 was accompanied by a severe drought in the region. Sanders soon went bankrupt, mostly because the local farmers couldn't pay him for the gas they'd bought on credit. To pay the final month's rent on the property, he was forced to begin selling the station's prized furnishings.

Sanders, as he already had done a number of times, simply shrugged and began looking for work once again.

Some of Harland Sanders's Careers

Farm hand	Insurance salesman
Street car conductor	Steamboat ferry operator
Under-age soldier	Tire salesman
Railroad fireman	Service station operator
Lawyer	Hotelier

A Dining Legend Is Born

Fortunately, his reputation was such that Shell Oil offered to build him another gasoline station and let him operate it rent-free at a location of his choice. Sanders chose Hell's Half Acre just outside of Corbin, Kentucky.

In 1930, Hell's Half Acre had no electricity, was a hotbed for moonshine activities and had a reputation for violence, particularly on Saturday nights. It didn't matter. Sanders saw only the opportunity, first for a gasoline station and then for a restaurant. He believed he could fill cars with gas and weary travelers with food at the same time.

His instincts about location would prove nearly as infallible as his instincts about food. When the station finally opened, he was approached by an itinerant sign-painter who proposed placing a few signs in the area, advertising Sanders's establishment. Sanders politely demurred, saying he didn't even have the money to pay for his first shipment of gas. But the hungry painter persisted and offered to paint the barns within a hundred-mile radius anyway—Sanders could pay him as the money came in.

"His price was so daggone low I couldn't afford not to do it. So I told him to go ahead. And just about every time he come back from painting new signs, our gasoline sales went up."
—Harland Sanders

The new station was set just off U.S. Route 25, then the main route between the tire manufacturers in Akron and the fabrics from Southern mills. Soon, Sanders was making a good living at the station—and, as he had suspected, the steady stream of truckers along U.S. 25 needed food as well as gasoline.

"I had a little room in the corner of the service station about fifteen-foot square that was used just for storage," Sanders recalled in his book *Finger Lickin' Good*. "It had rough planks for a floor. I went and got me a piece of linoleum for sixteen dollars on credit from the hardware store downtown. I put that on the floor and wheeled the old family dinin' room table into the space. We had six chairs, so that was our restaurant seating capacity."

Truckers, their stomachs growling, began arriving in droves. Word quickly got around about the quality of food, and the Sanders family—son, daughters, and their father—were soon cooking in shifts to feed the hungry public. Harland changed the name of his establishment from "Sanders Service Station" to "Sanders Service Station & Café," and eventually to "Sanders Café & Service Station."

Despite the area's rough-and-tumble reputation (it was a hotbed of illegal distilling activities, and at least one shootout between rival bootleggers erupted on his property), Sanders became deeply involved in life in Corbin.

As Sanders's business blossomed, so did his generosity. He would not charge a minister for food or accommodations. Once when his own bank account was shriveling, he impulsively gave a struggling orphanage a $750 check, only to be saved by two unexpected calls from traveling religious groups that for days filled his motel and restaurant—and his coffers.

When a four-room "tourist cottage" next door to the service station became available, Sanders leased it as well. The new Sanders Court & Café was a family affair. Sanders cooked, worked the cash register, and floated between the restaurant and the service station. Harland Jr., still in high school, helped pump gas and change tires, while young Mildred did a little of everything. Margaret helped, too, during breaks in her schooling.

Sanders had an obsession that was somewhat uncommon among his peers in the tourist trade—cleanliness. Travelers who had long suffered through a gauntlet of "greasy spoon diners" and mildew-stained cottages were drawn

> *"I hope to be a perfectionist as near as I can be, as best as I can be. That's what I've been demanding through the years."*
> —Harland Sanders

to Sanders Court because it was so thoroughly clean.

He once even angrily closed his restaurant when the staff didn't meet his demanding expectations. Daughters Margaret and Mildred both admitted that their father was a perfectionist. Sanders had to concur, adding that he never expected anything of anybody else that he didn't first expect of himself.

This passion for cleanliness never wavered, and it remained a cornerstone of his personal value system as long as he was actively involved in food service.

A Kentucky Colonel is Knighted

"Our restaurant still looked very crude on the outside, but word got around that the food was good on the inside," Margaret Sanders has written. "Gov. Ruby Laffoon heard about it and whooped up a lot of excitement when he arrived in his long limousine escorted by two motorcycle policemen. He soon became a regular customer and a good friend of the family."

Laffoon was impressed with the motel's "no-tipping policy," free newspapers, umbrella service when it rained, and the placing of tarps over automobiles at night during inclement weather. And for those only interested in a meal, Sanders had a replica of one of his motel rooms situated in a corner of the dining room.

One morning, after a satisfying meal at the restaurant, Laffoon sat at one of the solid maple tables adorned with neat red-checkered tablecloths and named Sanders an honorary "Kentucky colonel." Sanders embraced the title and, from that point on, was known almost exclusively as "the Colonel."

As business grew, the Colonel began to hire outside employees, first the husband-and-wife team of Nell and George Ray, then a young single mother with two children, Claudia Ledington Price. She would come to play an integral role both in the success of Kentucky Fried Chicken and in the life of Harland Sanders.

The Colonel began dreaming of a chain of restaurants, and by 1937 he had establishments in Cumberland and Richmond. Both of them failed, however, largely because he had hired too much staff for the minimal volume of trade the restaurants generated in those two depression-stricken towns, but also because Sanders himself was not present to "ride herd on the help."

By 1939, however, the Colonel's other businesses (including a furniture store and a plumbing store in Corbin) were doing so well that he built a second motel in Asheville, North Carolina, about ninety miles away. Claudia operated the motel, but, because of the seasonal nature of Asheville's tourism, it never prospered.

Also in 1939, Sanders Court & Café became one of the few restaurants in rural America listed in Duncan Hines's influential publication, *Adventures in Good Eating.* In response, the Colonel erected one of the largest signs in Northern Kentucky and, still with an early eye toward expansion, bought an interest in yet more restaurants in Berea and Asheville.

Perfecting Kentucky Fried Chicken

Later that year, when an electrical fire burned his original restaurant and part of the motel in Corbin to the ground, he decided to build a much larger restaurant in its place.

> *"I got to thinkin' to myself, you can sleep a man only once in twenty-four hours, but you can feed him three times."*
> —Harland Sanders

"So now, I built a fine new restaurant to seat 140 people," the Colonel recalled. "And that experience taught me one important lesson. That is, that my future from that point on was to be in food and food service, not in the motel business."

When the new, expanded restaurant opened on July 4, 1940, among the Colonel's many specialties was his Graham Cracker Cream Pie, soon legendary along the famed "Dixie Highway." Longtime patron W. S. McCracken remembered the "elegant way he operated his business and personally greeted his customers. (The Colonel's) was the only place in the area where shrimp, oysters, and other exotic seafood could be obtained on short order."

A collection of letters from former patrons of the Colonel's emphasizes one of the hallmarks of any restaurant he operated—his insistence that each customer be greeted warmly and

personally. It was another practice he never failed to honor throughout his life.

Cooking Under Pressure

Few restaurants offered Southern-style fried chicken in those days. Pan-frying took at least thirty minutes, and if he fried chicken in advance, too much might be left over at the end of the day. French frying was a faster but less palatable option. It meant immersing chicken in the same deep fat used for fries, which resulted in dry, crusty, and unevenly done chicken.

The solution to this dilemma was the original Presto pressure cooker introduced to the Colonel by a local hardware salesman. Sanders was an immediate convert to pressure cooking and bought seven more the following day. Much to the dismay of his cooks, the Colonel then spent months experimenting in their kitchens with various foods, including fried chicken.

The Colonel's Precise Formula

► Dip the chicken in a wash of eggs and milk.
► Roll the chicken in a flour seasoned with the Colonel's blend of herbs and spices.
► Pre-fry for a few seconds.

The Colonel began offering fried chicken cooked with his own special recipe on the menu at his restaurant. It soon became a popular item, although the Colonel was not yet satisfied with the blend of ten herbs and spices.

Setbacks and Heartache

The World War II years were difficult for the Sanders family on several fronts. Harland Jr. died of a strep infection that turned into endocarditis following a minor surgical procedure. The Colonel's restaurant in Asheville failed, his investments in new airports for Corbin and nearby London were costly failures, and in 1947 Josephine, his wife of thirty-seven years, finally filed for divorce. The Colonel married Claudia Price in 1949. He said that she became the soul mate he'd craved all of his adult life.

Still, the Colonel persevered. Sanders Court's country ham, hot biscuits, and honey were regional favorites. When Kentucky Gov. Earle Clements began the Governor's Tour in 1948, Sanders was on it. He made sure the busloads of touring business leaders stopped at his place, where he stuffed them with fried chicken and taught them how to make mint juleps (although Sanders himself never touched the stuff).

During and following the war, The Colonel became interested in politics, once stumping Kentucky for "Happy" Chandler, who would later become both a United States senator from Kentucky and commissioner of Major League Baseball. It was while working for Chandler that the Colonel first met John Y. Brown Sr., whose son would play a pivotal role in the KFC saga in years to come.

Sanders ran for Kentucky state representative in 1950–1951 on the "wet ticket" in a day when most rural counties prohibited the sale of alcoholic beverages. Sanders believed that the "wet ticket" would end the illegal and often deadly bootlegging of "moonshine whiskey." He also vowed to support a vigorous road-building program in the mostly poor mountain counties.

The Colonel lost by 187 votes. He later said that those 187 votes were "the best votes ever cast."

The Secret behind the Secret

After his brief flirtation with politics, the Colonel went back to his first love—constantly experimenting in his kitchen, looking for just the right combination of herbs and spices to flavor the batter of his fried chicken.

In 1950, he was asked to cater meals for a tour boat junket with five hundred people that docked at nearby Noe's Landing on the Cumberland River. It was then that he made a pragmatic but far-reaching decision. He always had been reluctant to try an eleventh spice because the current unnamed recipe had been so popular, but he seized a golden opportunity.

"Well, those folks are not my regular customers anyway, so I'm gonna try out this little change in the herbs and spices. I thought of this one herb I hadn't been using, and I knew right off (from their reactions that) I had the right combination."

According to daughter Margaret, it was the addition of an eleventh spice that created the magic. "One day," she recalls, "I said, 'Father, this is it. *This* is the taste. It is so good. You cannot beat this. It's universal.' So he took me back into the spice room. And above the doorjamb, he wrote the eleven herbs and spices that he put in that day. And he said, 'Nobody will look up here. Nobody will see this. You're the only one who will know it. So if anything happens to me, then you can make exactly the same taste I did, and you can go into business.'"

Whether he consciously knew it or not, the concept of a "secret recipe" chicken was a natural. John Y. Brown Jr. later called it "a brilliant marketing ploy." The pairing of a secret recipe and the intensely flavorful chicken itself proved to be an unbeatable combination.

The fried chicken was a resounding success with the tour boat and the Colonel always claimed to have never varied from the new recipe after that triumph.

Meanwhile, Sanders had been cultivating his "Colonel" image and slowly assembled what he considered proper accoutrements—the white linen suit, the string tie, and the goatee and mustache (both dyed white at first at Lo's Beauty Shop until his hair naturally turned a silver-white). He modeled himself after the editorial cartoons and caricatures he'd seen of Kentucky colonels as a young man.

The Origin of an Idea

It was during this period that he conceived the idea of peddling "Col. Sanders' secret recipe." Often, at slack times in the restaurant, he would visit other local restaurants, hoping they would consider featuring his chicken on the menu. Then, in 1951, as they had every year for the past decade, the Colonel and Claudia—"the Colonel's Lady"—attended a workshop hosted by the National Restaurant Association in Chicago.

In Chicago, the Colonel was appalled by the amount of alcohol consumed by the restaurant owners attending the convention. He and Claudia were soon attracted to a clean-cut couple from Salt Lake City, Pete Harman and his wife, Arline. Despite their age differences (the Colonel was sixty-one, Harman was thirty-two), they were immediately drawn to each other and struck up an instant—and enduring—friendship.

After the convention, the Colonel and his wife hit the road. "Claudia and me got up a sort of act," the Colonel said later. "We'd go into a restaurant, and she'd wear the old-time dress, you know, the hoop-skirt affair, and I'd be in my Colonel outfit, and she'd serve the chicken. When I was done in the kitchen, I'd come out and mingle with the guests."

But the Colonel and Claudia faced rejection after rejection while looking for restaurants that would franchise their recipe. Undeterred, the Colonel continued to try to sell his recipe of various herbs and spices and other cooking paraphernalia in the back seat of his car. Claudia often remained in Corbin, mixing up the packets of spices.

"I was glad when a restaurant owner invited me to have a meal with him," the Colonel wrote much later. "He didn't know it, but often I'd say goodbye to him at closin' time, fool around with my gear in the back of the car until he left, then climb in the back seat and get as comfortable as I could and sleep the rest of the night."

The Fateful Stopover

The Colonel nursed a lifelong dream of visiting Australia as well as an obsessive desire to "quit cussing." Somehow, by attending the International Church Conference of Christians, visiting Australia while surrounded by "well-spoken" clergymen, he thought he had found the answer to both. He also arranged a stopover in Salt Lake City to visit Pete Harman, another obvious good influence.

> *"Father was perennially concerned with his inability to stop cussing, and paralyzed with fear that he might go to hell for it."*
> —Margaret Sanders

The Colonel called Harman, hoping that Pete would offer him a room and an opportunity to promote his secret recipe chicken.

"Of course I didn't tell him that my reason for going was to try to get some inspiration to overcome my cussin', " the Colonel said. But Harman did offer a night's free lodging, so when the appointed day came, the Colonel took the train to Salt Lake City.

Pete Harman, a Born Leader

Leon "Pete" Harman's story has superficial similarities to the life of Harlan Sanders. Both lost their fathers early, both emerged from poverty, and both succeeded through hard work and enormous personal integrity.

But Pete Harman's model was his Aunt Carrie, a heroic, almost mythic figure in his life, a woman who alone raised fourteen children in the depths of the Depression and endowed her adopted son with a set of principles that enabled him to become KFC's first and eventually largest franchisee.

Her daily mantra—"Somehow we'll do it, by the principles of thrift, honor, integrity and charity"—impacted all of Pete's decisions from an early age. And that profoundly simple formula is the bedrock upon which Harman Management Corporation was founded. From that foundation, Pete built the beginnings of a culture that predicated personal success on the success of others and a lifetime of generous giving to a host of worthy causes.

Always give back to your community.

Because of Aunt Carrie, that generosity has been a commitment and an integral part of a supremely successful company from its earliest beginnings.

Aunt Carrie's Legacy

If we are, indeed, creatures of our environment, then Leon W. "Pete" Harman had little choice in life but to be generous to a fault, self-sacrificing, and a motivator of his "fellow man" (and woman). A single figure dominates Harman's life—his preternaturally selfless Aunt Carrie. Even now, when Pete speaks of her, more than sixty years after her passing, he's still moved to tears.

Among the Harman family files is a typewritten family history by an unknown author. The cover features a photograph of Aunt Carrie and a passage from "Ecclesiasticus" from *The Aprocrypha* (sic):

> *"Let us now praise famous men (women) . . . Leaders of the people by their counsels . . . Such as found out musical tunes, and recited verses in writings: Rich men (women) furnished with ability . . . All these were honoured in their generations, and were the glory of their times . . . that their praises might be reported.*
>
> *"And some there be, which have no memorial; who are perished as though they had never been; and are become as though they had never been born . . . But these were merciful men (women), whose righteousness hath not been forgotten . . . The people will tell of their wisdom and the congregation will shew forth their praise."*

And the person receiving the most praise is Aunt Carrie Harman.

The "Ecclesiasticus" history states that brothers George and David Harman came to the mostly Mormon village of Granger, Utah, in 1891 to work on Lachoneus "Cone" Hemenway's orchards. George married Hemenway's eldest daughter Caroline in January 1895; David married Grace in September 1898. Both sets of newlyweds bought land and settled in Granger.

According to this record, George caught a cold working in his irrigation canal in 1912 that soon turned into pleurisy. In his final days, he begged his brother David, "If anything happens to me, please look after Carrie and the children."

"David once made a similar request of George as he left (November 24, 1909) for a two-year mission when Grace was expecting their sixth child." (*Ecclesiasticus*)

George died on August 12, leaving Caroline to support their six children on the family farm.

"Each day she rose at 5:00 am, not only to tend to household duties, but also to work in the fields and orchards, teaching and training her young family," the "Ecclesiasticus" history records. "During the weekly irrigation turns, she and her sons would make beds in the wagon, hitch up the horses, drive to the fields, and set the water. Three or four times during the night, Caroline would awaken the boys and help them 'change' the water. Only during haying season did they hire work done."

In addition to their family responsibilities, the family history details that sisters Caroline and Grace also met weekly during World War I to knit sweaters for soldiers, roll bandages, and prepare other Red Cross supplies for shipment overseas. In 1917, Caroline was asked to become the president of the Relief Society in the Granger Ward—which then consisted of 822 members, including twenty-two widows.

The following year, David and Grace built a sprawling home large enough to accommodate their eight children, with the ninth on the way—named Leon Weston Harman—soon dubbed "Pete" by the family.

"I was born in Salt Lake City, in our home," Pete Harman recalled. "On January 16, 1919, during the depths of the influenza epidemic. About eight million people died that winter in the United States. Right after I was born, my mother also died of the flu. She was buried in a public cemetery."

> "Somehow we'll do it, by the principles of thrift, honor, integrity, and charity."
> —Aunt Carrie

Pete, just six hours old, was taken in by Caroline—or Aunt Carrie, as she was now called.

Carrie Harman's Relief Society, which had sewn the burial clothing, lined caskets, draped the chapel podium, and fed and comforted Granger's bereaved, now assumed those duties for Grace's family.

A month later, Aunt Carrie's oldest daughter, Annie, eight months pregnant, died of influenza. The family history claims that her health "broke" at the loss of her daughter and she sequestered herself in her bedroom:

"Weeks later, she arose from her bed, calm and determined. The doctor diagnosed her illness as sugar diabetes. From that time forth, she gave herself three insulin shots daily and carefully weighed her food."

To this day, Harman believes that it was Aunt Carrie who imbued all of her children with an extra measure of her indomitable will.

On October 29, 1919, David married his brother's widow Caroline in the Salt Lake Temple. The two families—now totaling fourteen children—moved into the sprawling house at 3600 West and 4100 South in Granger and the "Ecclesiasticus" records that it soon became the neighborhood meeting grounds for dozens of other children:

"The Harman home was a haven for hungry teenagers who liked the noise, the laughter, the impromptu dances, and the rollicking radio parties . . . while drinking cocoa (with lots of milk) from a quart jar."

Harman has only fragmentary memories of his father.

"The neighbors used to tell me what a great guy my father was," Pete said. "That was important to me. I know he was a farmer. He went on a Mormon mission to Tennessee when he had four or five kids. Number five was born while he was gone, because they go for two and a half years.

"I can remember how he would raise hay, bale it, and haul it to the city for the Livery Stables, and sometimes he'd bring some bananas home."

David and Carrie Harman managed the farm and orchards and became partners in the Relief Society. But David died just five years later, leaving Aunt Carrie twice-widowed with fourteen children.

Undeterred, Aunt Carrie grimly carried on. According to Harman, she was a woman of extraordinary strength—and faith. A devout member of the Church of Jesus Christ of Latter-Day Saints, she was the almost supernatural force behind the local Mormon Relief Society for eighteen years in Granger.

> *"In the lean years of the Great Depression, Aunt Carrie was everywhere, feeding the hungry, nursing the sick, raising money for the impoverished—all the while caring for the fourteen children under her roof."*
>
> —Pete Harman

"There was always food on the table, since we did have a farm," Harman said, "But as far as cash went, there was practically none. Poor? We weren't poor. We had food to eat. I never had a bad day in my life."

The family history also waxes eloquent about Aunt Carrie's reserves of strength and patience:

"How did she do it all with her large family? She did it with her large family. Day in day out, month after month, year after year, the Harman sons and daughters drove her in a horse and buggy led by Old Rose (and later in a car) to visit every home in the ward—many times. Her black buggy would go to the houses of those who had 'enough to spare.' At these homes she would gather goods and deliver them to the homes of those who had little or nothing.

"The Harmans were never idle. Before losing land prior to and during the Depression, they farmed 180 acres of dry farm and about one hundred acres irrigated. The sons and the daughters worked on the farm—plowing fields, sowing seeds, irrigating, harvesting hay and grain, sorting apples and potatoes, feeding chickens, pigs, cows, and horses."

Harman said Aunt Carrie's frequently spoken motto— "Somehow we'll do it, by the principles of thrift, honor, integrity and charity"—quickly became engrained in his young persona. He recalled that while caring for her own family, she would typically bake eight loaves of bread in a day, wash four loads of laundry and "can fruits and vegetables by the ton."

Even little Pete, the youngest and apparently most lavishly spoiled with attention from his older siblings, had chores:

"You start feeding the pigs and then, when you get older, you milk the cows," he said. "We usually had about five cows. Then when you get a little older still, you separated the milk. Then you would put it in a can and the dairy would pick up the cream. That would give us money to buy whatever we had to have.

"We had a common pasture where we would put cows out and leave them for two or three months in the summer. One day, a certain cow had a calf, so we went out, got the cow, and drove it in. It was an ornery bugger. Somebody had to milk it and, as the youngest, I was nominated. So I tied it up and tried, but it just kicked the hell out of me.

"I couldn't have been more than ten or twelve at the time, but I didn't give up. I studied the situation until I figured out what to do. I tied her horns with a rope to one post and her two hind legs to another post behind me—then I went and milked that cow. For some reason, that bonded us. Eventually, that cow would just wander free. She could eat anything she wanted in all the ditch banks. When milking time came, all I had to do was go out and holler 'Moo, moo' and that cow would come up to me on the corner steps, I would milk the cow sitting right there.

"One of the saddest days was when I needed money to buy clothes to go to school. I sold the cow—they gave me a lot of money for it, a lot more money than it was worth, really. But I had to lead the cow down to her new home and that was a sad, sad day."

Aunt Carrie eventually remarried in early 1925. Her new husband was sixty-six-year-old Eugene Robinson. Pete recalled Robinson as a "fine man."

But shortly after their marriage, Robinson suffered a stroke and was bed-ridden. Aunt Carrie and the children cared for him until his death in October 1930.

Outside of family and chores, Harman's life revolved around school and his church. His great-grandmother had been a Mormon pioneer, coming with Brigham Young in a handcart.

Aunt Carrie raised her family in the Mormon faith. For Pete, the Sunday schedule is still indelibly etched in his mind:

"You go to Sunday School and, when you reach twelve years old, you pass the Sacrament—that's the bread and water. Then when you get a little older, you can bless the Sacrament. That was a big deal."

There were other activities for young Mormon boys like little Pete Harman, including the church-sponsored Farm Bureau Baseball League.

"We found an old first baseman's glove in junior high school, so I was a first baseman. I was pretty good, not real good, but pretty good."

One childhood memory made a vivid impression on the young boy. Following Robinson's death, Aunt Carrie began selling eggs to augment the family's income. The family depended on Grandpa Hemenway's old Model T Ford to deliver the eggs and chicks. But when it broke down, there was no money to fix it.

"That Ford sat in the old garage," Pete said. "Everybody else whose car would break down and needed a part, a generator or whatever, would come here and get what they needed. It was pretty well stripped."

One day, Granger was battered by a high wind:

"The baby chickens had just been delivered the day before and the wind was just blowing like mad. The chicken coop was damaged and the wind was blowing the chicks all over the yard. We ran out, got the chickens, put them in the boxes, took them in the house and put them in the parlor on the floor. When we got done counting, we still had our five hundred chickens— and nowhere to keep them.

"When we got up the next morning, a truck pulled up with a bunch of lumber and about fifteen guys from the Mormon church. Without saying anything, they put that chicken coop back together. That kind of thing leaves an impression on you."

According to Harman Management chairman of the board and CEO, Jackie Trujillo, Pete Harman's generous nature was indeed ultimately shaped both by Granger's tightly knit community and Aunt Carrie's selfless devotion to others.

"Pete's told me over the years that Aunt Carrie was such a good influence on him," Trujillo said. "She molded him to be who is because she let him do his own thing. He says, 'I came home with some pretty scary ideas sometimes' And she would just ignore it. She would let him go and do it and make his own mistakes. She supported him 100 percent.

"It was in Granger where he learned how to work, where he learned integrity, where he learned to how to get along with people—it was just a basic pioneer philosophy."

Harman attended elementary school in Granger, but by the time he got to ninth grade, school was offering fewer and fewer attractions.

One intriguing—and perhaps prophetic—story from Harman's school days was reported by Norman Vincent Peale in one of his widely syndicated columns from 1972. After recounting Harman's hardscrabble family life, Peale jumped the narrative to Pete's junior high school days:

"When he was in the eighth grade, he missed school for five days and had been guilty of some other infraction of the rules. The school principal, called him into his office, and said a surprising thing. 'You know, Pete, you've got amazing potential within you. Did you ever hear of the "personality-expansion" factor? Well, you've got it and I mean plenty. You're a natural-born leader. On the bad side, I've got to remind you that you're headed the wrong way.

"'So you are now where you must choose between two directions. You could be one of the worst criminals of our time or one of the most constructive leaders of our time. Think it over.'"

Despite the unnamed principal's best efforts, Harman's educational experience was still ambivalent at best. He did well in mathematics, but poorly in English—although his favorite teacher was Ann Pearson, the English teacher, who lived to see his later success.

22

But there was little work for fifteen-year-old Pete Harman in Granger. And by the tenth grade, he looked restlessly beyond the mountains. He quit school and worked first as a grocery clerk and later as a farm laborer, earning between twenty and thirty cents an hour, most of which he gave to Aunt Carrie.

When two of his older brothers moved to California in 1936, Harman impetuously took the remaining money from the sale of his beloved cow and hitchhiked to San Francisco.

A short stint working in a steel mill earned Harman seventy dollars. But when the mill laid him off, other jobs grew scarce as the Depression deepened.

"I got down to three bucks," he recalled. "Room rent was three bucks and for quite a while I would go out and look for jobs every morning. One day I went in John's Steak House on Golden Gate Avenue and Market Street. They had a very nice hostess and I said I wanted to talk to the manager. She wanted to know what I wanted. I said, 'I'd like a dishwasher's job, or any job, even if it's part-time.' She said, 'We haven't hired anyone here for three or four years. But let me buy your lunch.'

"I said, 'I don't want a free lunch. I want a job.'

"So she said, 'Wait a minute.' She phoned the business agent down at the union hall. 'There is a young man here I want you to hire,' she said. So that's how I got in the restaurant business."

Shortly thereafter, he took a job as an $18.67-a-week dishwasher in a restaurant called Foster's Lunch.

"It was a restaurant just like ours today," he said. "For some reason or another, our service today is just exactly the same. You take your tray to the counter and give your order. They hand it to you and you pay right there.

"I worked my way up. And when I was twenty years old, I was a night manager of a store with a bunch of fifty-year-old cooks."

Arline, the Light of Pete's Life

At nights, Harman could be found at the famed Avalon Ballroom, a popular dance hall in San Francisco.

"They danced seven nights a week there," Pete said. "The band had four guys and a good-looking gal singer.

"I took five dollars worth of dancing lessons with a nice lady who was fifteen years older than I was. I danced with her. We made a couple of rounds around the dance floor and I caught on. The fast dance was a fox trot and the slow one was a waltz.

"She said, 'Don't waste your money on dance lessons—you can dance!'"

One night, there was a new girl on the dance floor at the Avalon Ballroom, Arline Hampton, a "candy girl" who lived with her aunt and worked in the Ferry Building. She was joined by three friends but, according to Harman, she was by far the prettiest.

"I danced with her on her first night at the Avalon," Harman recalled. "She walked up, very early in the evening, and said, 'Let's dance.'"

Pete was immediately smitten. Although naturally shy, he still thought he had a chance with the girl who looked like a young Barbara Stanwyck.

"Well, I had a car. Willie Taylor bought this '36 Ford and he couldn't afford the payments. He let another guy take over the payments and he couldn't afford the payments, but I had enough money to take over the payments. They made a good-looking car. It was a good car. And if you had a car, you could get girls to go out with you."

Soon Pete and Arline were inseparable. He quickly proposed.

"But her family was not happy," he said. "They thought they were pretty high-powered. So I just invited them the night of the wedding. I phoned up a Christian preacher at random—we'd never even seen him before—we went up in his office and got married. So they knew that I had a mind of my own when we got done."

Three months after their initial dance, on January 19, 1938, Pete and Arline were married. Pete was nineteen; Arline was twenty-one.

When he heard about the wedding, Arline's father just shook his head and told his daughter, "Oh, you married a 'hasher' (fry cook), did you?"

Like Pete, Arline had endured a Spartan childhood before ending up in San Francisco in 1936.

"I was born in Lincoln, Nebraska in 1916. The next thing I remember was my dad and mom separated. I lived with my mother after that. It was kind of hard on her because she didn't have a trade, so she worked as a housekeeper. Lots of times we would have to go out of town. She would answer ads in the paper. That was kind of scary, but she had to do it. I got so that I just hated to start school. I used to cry if I had to start another school without knowing anybody."

Later, Harman would joke that Arline married him for his money. At the time, she was making fifty cents an hour, while he had been promoted to 67-½ cents an hour at Foster's Coffee Shop in San Francisco, California.

The Harmans' first child, Barry, was born in August 1939. When Barry was six months old, Arline joined Pete at Foster's as a waitress.

Aunt Carrie's Legacy

Back in Granger, Aunt Carrie's children had all finally left home, so she turned her considerable energy to raising chickens. But unknown to most of the family, her adult onset diabetes had resulted in gangrene.

One evening, she told a friend, "I can face my sister Grace because I know that I did all she would have done if I had been called away and she had stayed. I have no regrets. In some ways all the children could do better. And they will. We taught them right."

On the evening of July 29, 1940, following a ride with daughter Marjory, she died in her home. Her last words were, "I'd like to rest now."

The funeral was one of the largest ever held in Granger, filling the Granger Ward House. Although Aunt Carrie had out-lived many of her contemporaries, family and friends came from three states to honor her. Harman said that her eulogy was delivered by Bishop Bangerter, whose son would later become governor of Utah.

"My Aunt Carrie raised me," Pete said. "She had super-high principles. She was always out helping. Anybody got sick in the community—she'd be there, helping. You wanted to succeed for her.

"I don't think anybody really wants to succeed for himself if he or she can make other people successful.

"I have two mothers. My birth mother and Aunt Carrie. My Aunt Carrie did more for more people than anybody I know. And she did more for me than she did for anyone else. She had every reason to be waited on. Yet she continually served others. She never complained. She never quit. Aunt Carrie asked little of life. She asked little and gave much. And she was happy with what she had.

"Like many other aunts we never hear about, she was all service and no quit.

"Whoever I am today was because she took care of me."

Moving Up, Moving On

Pete and his small family sadly returned to San Francisco. But the Harmans thrived in pre-war San Francisco and Pete's initiative was soon spotted by Foster's management. Eventually, he became the night manager. All seemed well, but in 1941 a second funeral service, this time for a family friend, changed their lives.

"When we were still working in San Francisco, we went back for another funeral in Salt Lake," Pete said, "my sister's baby died. There was no cold rain, no fog. It seemed that Utah had everything that California didn't have. Arline said, 'Boy, I'd sure like to live there.'"

Pete agreed. Later that year, they planned their first vacation as a couple—again to Salt Lake City. Meanwhile, Harman told his brother Jake that he'd like to go into business for himself in the Salt Lake City area—and to keep his eyes open for any prospects.

Somewhere in the ensuing lean years, Pete and the handsome '36 Ford he had courted Arline in had parted company. Instead, he was driving a '28 Buick he had borrowed from his friend Jack Abernathy. Harman recalled that the two had something of a "lend-lease" agreement—Pete and Arline could use the Buick indefinitely and Pete would periodically send Jack money whenever he had fifty dollars to spare.

Unfortunately, the car was stolen shortly after their arrival in Salt Lake City before Harman could make the first payment. (Jack forgave the debt, but Pete bought Jack a new station wagon thirty years later.)

Family photo albums feature pictures of a bare-chested Pete posing with their son Barry and a smiling Arline, also with Barry, standing in front of the Salt Flats en route to Salt Lake City. The couple had fifteen dollars between them— just enough for gas money to return to California.

Once in town, Pete again contacted his brother Jake, who ran a small fresh vegetable food stand.

"My brother wanted me to stay in Utah," Harman said. "He was the only one out of the nine kids who still lived in Salt Lake and he was lonesome.

"He pulled me aside and said, 'There is a little restaurant down here. I bet you could buy it very cheap because the old fellow is drinking himself to death.'"

The restaurant was called Erath's and the asking price was seven hundred dollars—with no money down—for a dirty little hamburger-and-root-beer joint at the corner of 39th South and State on the edge of Salt Lake City. It featured eight bar stools, five booths, three pinball machines, a juke box, a gravel drive-up for the carhops, and an outhouse.

Older brothers Jack and Morris Harman were instrumental in helping Pete arrange financing.

For a high school dropout with a family, Harman's career choices were limited at best.

"I had three options open to me—farming, railroading, or the unknown," he said. "I took the unknown—the restaurant business—mainly because I'd gotten pretty good at it at Foster's in San Francisco."

With Arline's blessing, they closed on the deal.

"We bought it for very little and agreed to make some kind of a payment weekly," Harman said. "We thought we were getting along fine. But in order to get the power and the gas, we had to put down a deposit. Utah Power and Light averaged the three highest months of the year—when you were using the most power—and you had to pay one third of that as a deposit. But the gas guy said, 'I know you are going to do fine. I'll drive by from time to time and when you get enough to pay the deposit on the gas, flag me in.' So that is how we got our gas deposit."

The electricity deposit was another matter. Pete recalled that it was a whopping $125.

"'To get the deposit, another of my brothers had an old sugar beet truck that was paid for," Pete said. "It was the only thing he had that was paid for. We hocked that truck to get the deposit."

Pete and Arline stayed with friends Mig and Chic Palmer until they could afford a place of their own. It took two weeks to find an apartment—in a nearby two-room motel. The Harmans lived in the little motel their entire first year in Salt Lake City.

Meanwhile, they cleaned up the small root beer stand as best they could and opened for business on Labor Day 1941.

The Do Drop Inn

"The first day I was in business, a match salesman came in," Harman said. "I figured every big operator that paid seven hundred dollars for a location had to have his own book matches. So we paid seven dollars for a case of matches.

"We had one problem—the match salesman wanted to know the name of our place. Well, it was so junky I didn't want to put my name on it. The salesman said, 'The Dew-Drop Inn is always good.' So that's where the name came from. Arline didn't like it too much, but when we dignified it enough to spell it 'Do Drop' instead of 'Dew-Drop,' she went for it."

The first day's receipts were meager—about thirteen dollars—and not nearly enough to cover the restaurant's monthly rent of eighty dollars or the fifty-dollar license fee, much less living expenses.

Pete was the last to leave, slowly locking up the restaurant. When he went to the storeroom to close up, the wall was covered with cockroaches.

Harman said that Aunt Carrie had always drilled the importance of cleanliness in him. Acting quickly, he grabbed a handy bottle of fly spray and sprayed the wall.

The next morning, he was the first to arrive. He went to the storeroom and began cleaning up the piles of dead roaches, which now littered the floor. As he bent over to sweep up the last pile, he saw Chauncey Millen, the iceman, standing in the doorway.

"I said, 'Do you think I'll ever make a living for my family in this place?' And he very seriously said, 'Clean the damn place up and you'll do fine.' And I did."

Harman made cleanliness his focus in the days that followed. Soon, the dingy old restaurant sparkled. It wasn't pretty, but it shined. Customers noticed—and returned.

And Chauncey the iceman also helped ensure that the little restaurant would survive by deferring payments until the young couple had a chance to earn a little more money.

Business Sense

When the second day's receipts at the Do Drop Inn were down by a couple of dollars, Pete took immediate action. He dropped the price of the fifteen-cent hamburger to two for fifteen cents.

"Business didn't seem to improve too much for the first two weeks," Pete said. "But we have always been very publicity-minded. So we phoned the neon sign company and contracted for a neon sign that cost $4,600—to be paid off on a three-year contract. The rent on the sign as was about three times as much as our rent on the building. But with two burgers for fifteen cents, we needed customers. We didn't really have the technical ability to run a very good place, although we thought we could make a pretty good hamburger at the time. And from that day on, after we installed that sign, business began to grow."

That decision, and many more like it in the years to come, are typical of Harman's instinctive grasp of marketing. Jackie Trujillo (now chairman of Harman Management) calls him a "marketing genius" and said that this small incident was indicative of Pete's grasp of the essentials of business.

> *"He acted swiftly when he realized the cash-flow wasn't going to be sufficient to cover expenses," she said. "Instead of cutting back when times got bad, he realized that he needed to increase his advertising, increase his exposure. Pete never took a marketing class in his life. But his business timing was always impeccable. He proved it time and time again."*

"That sign was our first entry into advertising," Harman said.

Pete was the primary cook. Arline, when she could get away, served as a hostess and waitress along with Mary Lees, a waitress they had "inherited" with the restaurant. The Do Drop Inn offered waffles (with ham or eggs) for forty cents, seventy-five cents for a chicken-fried steak with all of the trimmings, and of course, two hamburgers for fifteen cents.

It also offered draft beer for a dime a mug. But Harman, born and bred in Mormon Granger, had never tapped a keg.

"When our first keg ran out, I tried to put the new tap in as best I could," he said. "It ran out right in the middle of the night and the next morning I came in, whatever the hell I did wrong, beer went all over the ceiling. It was about half my inventory.

"Wally Anderson was the distributor and when he heard about it, he came and gave me a brand new barrel of beer.

"My brother's grocery store was struggling, too. A beer license cost a hundred dollars in those days. The day before July the first he would come over and give me a check for one hundred dollars and I would give him a check for a hundred dollars—and they were on different banks. Before they could clear, we had the Fourth of July, and we had the money to keep the license."

One lesson Harman still points to from his early days with the Do Drop Inn was that members of the food service community helped each other during tough times. Without that help, many would not have survived.

"I quickly saw that you didn't need to see other restaurants as competitors or your suppliers as adversaries," Harman said. "We're all in this together. I wanted these people do business with me again and again. It's a practice that's continued to serve us well."

For example, Harman said that business usually dried up to a trickle during Utah's frigid winters, but Zion's Wholesale Grocery, which supplied the Do Drop Inn, always extended credit until Pete's customers began to return, usually in May. Harman never forgot Zion's faith in him and the company remained his primary wholesaler for many years.

> *"In time, I saw that I wasn't in the food business – I was in the people business."*
> —Pete Harman

The War Years

The bombing of Pearl Harbor and the advent of World War II had a life-altering impact on every facet of American life—including the restaurant business. The government quickly instituted a rationing program of basic foodstuffs, strictly limiting the amount of staples like meat, bread, and sugar that both homeowners and restaurants could purchase.

Still, by the sheer force of their wills, Pete, Arline and their tiny staff turned the restaurant around. Harman recalled that at the end of the year, the Do Drop Inn saw a gross profit of $18,000.

"We ran the Do Drop Inn together and then we finally started building a business," Harman recalled. "Every time we would break a record on Friday night's sales, we would take the whole staff down to a Chinese restaurant and buy them chow mein, which cost sixty cents. You can't believe how they got onto that program. We went down at least six weeks in a row, because the waitresses would get all their friends to come in there and eat. That was one of our first incentive programs."

When the Harmans' second child, Dawn, was born on June 10, 1943, Arline's time in the restaurant dwindled even further. Fortunately, that coincided with the Do Drop Inn's increasing success, which allowed Pete to hire more help.

Each succeeding year, the Harmans would plow most of the profits back into the little Do Drop Inn, expanding it slightly, adding more features, upgrading the facilities. The first year's remodel entailed a new stucco finish, pale green paint and oval windows.

The first year's gross was enough that Pete felt comfortable enough to hire a second full-time waitress, Nila Washam. A Salt Lake City native, Nila worked several jobs, including a stint working for a private detective, before joining the Do Drop Inn in 1944. She was an instant hit with the customers, whom she invariably called "pumpkin" or "dear." Soon, customers asked for her by name.

> *"You've got to do a little more than the next guy if you want to come out better than him."*
> —Pete Harman

In the fall of 1944, Pete was drafted at the age of twenty-five. He served for just over two years at Camp Roberts in California. Pete was an eager but inexperienced soldier and was quickly "wounded" on the parade field during the endless marching drills.

"My feet hurt and I went up to the PX to get some medicine for them," he said. "The PX had a doctor who looked at my feet and said, 'I want you to come back here tomorrow and we'll take some X rays of your feet.' As it turned out, the metatarsal bones had broken on both feet. Those suckers hurt! But I thought everybody's feet hurt. After that I worked in an office. I carried the mail for the battalion; I even had a bicycle.

"But on D-Day, when the Army suffered those huge losses on the beaches of Normandy, they sent the order out that every mailman needed to put their bags out in front of their barracks at 0600 hours—they are shipping everybody out.'

"I went over to see my sergeant and said, 'A buddy of mine and I have cars—how are we going to get rid of a car?' He said, 'Harman, damn it, I forgot to tell you. You are on furlough. I sent you home on furlough. So take off.' So we went to Salt Lake for a two-week furlough."

But it was back in Salt Lake City at the Do Drop Inn that Harman saw his only action of the war.

"In those days, we burned all the paper trash in the back," Pete said. "When I was on furlough, I went back to work. I was burning some trash when something exploded. It just burned the hell out of me. I went to the hospital and they wouldn't release me until I got better, about a month later.

"Finally, I went back to Camp Roberts and this same old sergeant of mine said, 'Hell, I just transferred you to Salt Lake!' Then he got on the telephone and put me back in Camp Roberts again."

The farm boy from rural Granger missed the outdoors while on the military base and eventually planted and nurtured a patch of green lawn to work on his suntan outside his barracks window.

One charming photo from Pete's otherwise uneventful tour of duty still exists. It features Pete on another furlough in his starched uniform with Arline, looking for all the world like Patty of the Andrews Sisters, enjoying themselves at Earl Carrol's Vanities in Los Angeles. The photograph is dated 1944.

But while Pete was delivering mail at Camp Roberts, Arline was left with two small children and a restaurant to run. In addition to Mary Lees, Pete's sister Eliza, his brother Bruce and two carhops operated the Do Drop Inn. Arline was forced to board Barry and Dawnie during especially busy weeks.

Arline frequently consulted with Pete on significant purchases, but made most of the decisions herself. Some choices were difficult—the restaurant was only allotted a certain number of "points" or "food stamps" to buy food. Some foodstuffs were rationed so heavily they were simply unavailable.

"Pete never took a marketing clas. in his life, but his business timing wa always impeccable. He proved it time and time again."

—Jackie Trujill Harman Management CEC

But other decisions were easy—prices were frozen during the war.

"You were really rationed on red meat," Harman recalled, "but chicken was among the few things that wasn't rationed.

"Every twenty-fourth of July, the Mormon community has a big parade in Salt Lake City. Everybody in Utah comes to see it. The only thing is that *every* restaurant closes up as well. I couldn't stand to see these poor little kids from St. George, Utah, five hours away, that were going hungry.

"So I decided to stay open. I talked to the Wonder Bread guy and he gave us a bunch of bread that some grocery stores should have gotten. You could buy mayonnaise—that wasn't rationed. We boiled I don't know how many eggs, smashed them up, put them as filling on the bottom, and added a leaf of lettuce on the top. We had cars lined up for at least three blocks because we were the only ones open.

"We built a lot of good will feeding them that day. I don't think we made a lot of money, but people talked about that for ten years later."

Arline made other important decisions while Pete was off winning the war. It was Arline who purchased the first sack of flour from Sherman D. Robinson of Lehi Roller Mills in 1946, beginning a relationship that continues to the present day.

And it was Arline who hired attorney Bill Burton to represent the Do Drop Inn's legal interests. The firm of McKay, Burton & Thurman has since handled all of the Harman's legal matters as well.

Harman's tour of duty was finally up in 1946. Working in the battalion's mail room, he was first to see all incoming orders. As the Army and Navy began to shrink back to peacetime size, overseas veterans were mustered out first. But family men with their own transportation were the second group released from their military commitment.

As always, Harman had somehow managed to secure a car, a battered sedan with three rows of jump seats. Once they were discharged, Harman and some buddies stowed their duffel bags and piled into the roadster. They drove non-stop from Camp Roberts to Salt Lake City.

"Once back in town, I found a local judge who was a friend of mine," Harman said. "He made the paperwork legal and I sold that old car to a couple of Army buddies from New Jersey who'd come with me—and off they went to the East Coast."

Arline, for her part, gratefully relinquished day-to-day operations of the Do Drop Inn and went back to her other full-time job, that of mother of two children.

"Arline kept things together," Harman said. "If it hadn't been for her, there wouldn't have been a job to come home to after the war. She put up with me working a lot of hours. I always did work a lot of hours."

The Postwar Boom

During the post-war economic boom, Harman decided to take advantage of it. The Do Drop Inn stayed open twenty-four hours and Pete hired two former Marines, Arch Coates and Bob Peterson, to handle the night shift. He added homemade, hand-cranked ice cream to the menu. And he ordered the cooks to grill onions day and night—their aroma designed to entice customers walking by the restaurant.

Pete and Arline continued to remodel and expand the Do Drop Inn each year. He also joined first the Utah Restaurant Association and then the National Restaurant Association in 1946. As money became available, he and Arline attended the NRA's national conventions.

"I always love going to National Restaurant Association meetings," Harman said.

"I'm always looking for ways to improve this business. I love seeing the new products and concepts—and, of course, running into old buddies."

Pete was a keen student of the restaurant business and attended as many seminars as possible—always watching for that extra something that would separate the Do Drop Inn from its competition.

Pete's Words of Wisdom

▶ Praise in public—reprimand in private.
▶ Parents love to hear the accomplishments of their children.
▶ There's no such thing as luck—you make your own damn luck.

Harman still worked thirteen-hour days at the restaurant, helping out on both sides of the counter, priding himself on his ability to remember the names and preferences of regular customers.

"You've got to do a little more than the next guy if you want to come out better than him," he said.

"The opportunities have always been around for young people who really have the desire and ambition to make it."

According to daughter Dawn, her father somehow flourished in the long hours:

"Probably one of my earliest memories is coming home from school and seeing him take a nap in the middle of the living room floor. And I got the clue when things were going better, because he moved to the couch."

In 1948, Pete became the charter president of the Granite Park Lions Club—his first experience in a leadership position outside the Do Drop Inn. Many of the original thirty-two members remained life-long friends.

A Bigger, Better Restaurant

At last, business out-grew the old root beer stand. On the tenth anniversary of opening the Do Drop Inn, Harman decided he needed a bigger restaurant.

"I went to the bank and said I wanted to build a new building right over the top of the old one—a nicer restaurant," Pete said. "Our banker said, 'Sure. But on one condition: change the name from the Do Drop Inn and we'll loan you $30,000.' I said, 'You got any ideas?' And he said, 'Well, it should either be Pete's or Harman's—take your pick and I will loan you the money.' We have done business with that banker ever since, and still do."

Miraculously, despite building the hundred-seat Harman Café atop the old Do Drop Inn, Pete said the restaurant never missed a day of service.

With the expansion, and a new carhop service, came the need for additional waitresses. Of the first three hirees, Nila Washam, Betty Allen, and Alice Hardy, Alice and Betty would eventually move into management positions at Harman's. In the years that would follow, the always popular Nila repeatedly refused promotions.

"I just liked waiting tables," she once said. "I didn't want to get into the management end of the thing, to take on that extra responsibility. I just wanted to keep on giving all my customers the best service they could get anywhere in the city."

(In 1978, Nila would win an award from Kentucky Fried Chicken's *Bucket* magazine for her thirty-three years of service to Pete Harman, honoring her as the second oldest employee of KFC—she was the oldest person next to the Colonel.)

"Nila taught me most of what I know about working with people and doing a good job serving customers," Betty—herself a thirty-one-year employee at the time—told the *Bucket*. "She took me under her wing and showed me what to do back in those old days at the Do Drop Inn."

Business boomed. Hamburgers were now twenty-five cents. Pete sold what he called the Pedigree Hot Dog and Double

Header Hamburger—named for the Double Header train that regularly thundered down the nearby railroad tracks. On a good Saturday, Harman's cleared $1,000 in receipts.

But something still nagged at him.

"For some time, I'd been searching for a product I could introduce into my restaurant that would set it apart from other eateries," he once told *The Enquirer.*

Pete's restless nature took him back to the National Restaurant Association's annual convention in Chicago in 1951. They stayed in dorms at the University of Chicago by night and by day wandered the halls, looking at the exhibits, sampling dishes, attending classes, and meeting people. On one such foray, Pete and Arline met a distinguished gentleman from Kentucky named Harland Sanders.

"I first met the Colonel in a short course at the University of Chicago," Pete said. "It was a five-day course and he and Claudia were there. Most of the others were a bunch of Texas operators and they went out and got drunk every night. So the four of us went out to dinner three or four nights."

The main topic of conversation?

"Recipes—he was big on everything related to food," Pete recalled.

And on the final day of the seminars, the two couples parted company and returned home.

Pete's Words of Wisdom

▶ I don't think anybody really wants to succeed for himself if he or she can make other people successful.

▶ Nobody cares how much you know until they know how much you care.

3

A Simple Handshake

When Pete and the Colonel shook hands, they baptized KFC's first franchisee and together created an American icon. They also immediately established a serious, industry-changing precedent:

Franchisees bring a special passion and commitment to growing your business.

For Pete Harman (and those who followed him), the wellspring of his immediate success was his natural inclination to praise and promote his employees. As a result, from the beginning, the cream rose to the top, empowering Harman Management with an impressive stable of committed, imaginative leaders.

Those concepts—employee empowerment, recognition, and ownership—have been enthusiastically embraced by KFC and its parent company Tricon Global Restaurants as well, creating a much-envied corporate culture that has taken hold around the globe.

And its roots can be found in a simple handshake in Salt Lake City, more than fifty years ago!

Pete was trying to fix a light switch on a walk-in cooler at the Do Drop Inn when the Colonel slipped in and tapped him on the shoulder. It was August 3, 1952, and Harland Sanders was on his way to Australia with a stop-off in Salt Lake City to talk to the clean-cut young man he'd met and liked in Chicago.

Ever the friendly host, Pete took Sanders on a leisurely tour of the area—lunch at the Hotel Utah Roof Garden, a walk through the Mormon Temple grounds, and a trip to the Bingham Canyon Copper Mines sixteen miles away.

During the tour, Harman's offhand comment that his restaurant needed a food specialty to distinguish it from other hamburger joints set the Colonel's mind racing. Sanders knew he had the answer, but he struggled for a way to make the point with his newfound friend. It always had been a frustrating experience for the Colonel to convince others of the value of something that he believed in so fervently. He was looking for a break.

> *"This gravy's so good you can throw the chicken away and eat the gravy."*
> —Harland Sanders

He made his move on the last night of his visit with the Harmans. When Pete suggested dinner at a restaurant in the mountains above Salt Lake City, the Colonel said, "Pete, instead of you taking me up the canyon for dinner, I want to cook for you." He had a hint of desperation in his voice. Harman's response was cool, but Sanders began barking out orders.

He needed spices, he needed a pressure cooker, he needed chicken, and he needed a stove to cook on. They found spices and four whole chickens at Jake's grocery story. A pressure cooker was tracked down at Nila Washam's home, and she was invited to come try the new kind of chicken with them at about 5:30 that evening.

The Colonel was a whirlwind in the kitchen, but inadequate burners on the stove slowed him down. It took forever to boost the oil to the necessary four hundred degrees. As time ticked away and stomachs growled, the chicken finally was ready and put in a hot cabinet for holding until dinner. "Then I fried off the cracklings and made a kettle of cream gravy," said the Colonel. "Pete came by and asked what I was doing, and I said I'm making cream gravy that goes with the chicken. This gravy's so good you can throw the chicken away and eat the gravy."

"'Huh,' was all he said. He didn't even look to see how I was doin' it." Finally, at 10:00 PM, the Colonel announced that dinner was ready and set out the food for his dubious hosts. "It looks like greasy restaurant chicken," Arline whispered to Pete while the Colonel fussed some more in the kitchen. Then she began munching on her favorite morsel, a drumstick.

> *"She got the darndest gleam in her eye, and I knew it was good. It was so good we broke up the rolls to sop up the gravy."*
> —Pete Harman

The Colonel went on to San Francisco the following morning, then caught his flight to Australia. Two weeks later, Claudia met him in San Francisco, and the Colonel—his propensity for cussing still untamed—proposed that instead of flying straight to Kentucky, they take a train and see some of the beautiful vistas in the Rockies. Claudia also agreed to a quick stop along the way in Salt Lake City.

The persistent Colonel badly wanted firmer confirmation from the Harmans that they *loved* his fried chicken.

The First Kentucky Fried Chicken Restaurant

Like everyone else who had tried the Colonel's secret recipe, Harman *had* liked it. In fact, he'd *loved* the recipe so much that the day after the Colonel left Salt Lake for Australia, Harman bought several pressure cookers and called his sign painter, Don Anderson. "We'd built this restaurant with windows ten feet high and forty feet long," Harman said. "So I told Don to go out and paint a sign on those windows. We're going to put this chicken in." Don, of course, wanted to know what the signs should say—there was no name for the Colonel's chicken at the time.

"We thought of several names, including Utah Fried Chicken. But that didn't have much of a ring to it. Finally I said, 'I've never been to Kentucky, but to me Kentucky means Southern hospitality and good food.' Don asked, 'Why don't we name it Kentucky Fried Chicken?'"

And that was the name that appeared on Harman's restaurant August 4—and what greeted Colonel and Claudia when they stepped off the streetcar they had taken from the train station.

Kentucky Fried Chicken— Something New, Something Different

The Colonel's edited comment was, "I'll be daggoned." Harland Sanders had left Salt Lake City two weeks earlier unsure about putting his fried chicken in Harman's restaurant. "Now here he was tellin' all the city how good it was." A happy reunion of the two couples ensued.

> *"More than any other event in our early struggle to launch the idea of Kentucky Fried Chicken, Harman's acceptance of it and his enthusiasm in sharin' his experiences with other potential franchisees kept us going when we didn't have too much other success."*
>
> —Harland Sanders

Margaret Sanders wrote later about her father's pivotal meeting with Harman. "Harman," the Colonel said, "You've got good Mormons all over this state who would like this chicken. You live too far out West for me to get back here, but with your enterprising spirit, I know what you can do. I'm going to give you a franchise to develop the whole state of Utah using my secret recipe, and you'll never have to pay me a nickel in royalties." Harman and the Colonel cemented their new arrangement with a handshake.

> ## Pete's Words of Wisdom
>
> ► Do business with people as if you'd do business with them again.
> ► Learn from others. Pick the brains of experts and amateurs alike.
> ► Put a lot of effort in whatever you do. You earn what you get.
> ► Everybody does something damn good.

Moving on Two Fronts

After a quick visit to Pete's attorneys, McKay, Burton and Thurman, in Salt Lake City to trademark Kentucky Fried Chicken, a reinvigorated Colonel moved on to Washington, D.C., where he met with Margaret, who lived there at the time, and showed her a prototype of his proposed brochure.

"Daughter, don't you see?" she recalled him saying, "I could have something like this printed and take it along to the National Restaurant Convention in Chicago in October. The brochure would let everyone know I'm willing to give them a franchise to use my secret seasoning and my method of fast cooking."

Margaret, almost as impulsive as her father, volunteered to become his first employee. She moved back to Corbin in July 1954, with few belongings and 3,500 brochures in her trunk. Unfortunately, the brochures elicited few responses when the Colonel took them to Chicago. His typical reaction was to hit the road again, seeking restaurant owners with vision and cooks interested in his revolutionary new product. It was a tough sell.

At the same time, in Salt Lake City, there were more signs of progress. One of the first residents to actually eat Kentucky Fried Chicken from Harman's Café was local grocer Morris Worshaw, who had lunch there the day after the Colonel's departure. "I took him an order to try it," Harman recalled. "Then I said, 'What do you think about it? How much do you think we can sell?' He said something that probably changed the direction of our company. 'How much do you want to sell?' And, of course, I didn't know."

Worshaw said the answer was to advertise, because Harman had a very good product. "If you're gonna sell it, you're gonna have to advertise. How much you want to sell depends on how much you want to advertise." In subsequent years, Pete would frequently cite Morris's comment as one of the defining moments of Harman Management's ultimate success. But Jackie Trujillo cited an even more far-reaching consequence of the encounter:

"He doesn't have any preconceived notions. If an idea or concept strikes him as true, then he acts. It's that simple. Pete listens to people. In the case of advertising, he didn't wait a year to put an aggressive advertising campaign in next year's budget—he acted right then. As a result, Kentucky Fried Chicken was an immediate success."

> *"It typifies one of Pete's greatest strengths. He learns from people. He asks questions. He applies what he hears. Pete is forever picking the brains of experts and amateurs alike—sifting what he hears and putting it into action."*
> —Jackie Trujillo

The addition of the signature dish Harman had been searching for—the Colonel's chicken—prompted him to accelerate his advertising campaign. "We got in touch with the local radio station and asked them how much unsold time they had," Harman said. "It was a time of year that radio commercials weren't in demand, so we bought all the unsold time the station had—for five hundred dollars that month. And we probably had a thousand commercials. If there was any one thing that got Kentucky Fried Chicken off the ground, it was gambling on radio's unsold time. We had to change equipment practically every day for two weeks just to cook enough chicken to satisfy demand."

Kentucky Fried Chicken was an immediate hit. "Business just took off," Harman later told a *San Francisco Chronicle* reporter. "Before we knew it, we were in the chicken business, and people were lining up to get in. Within a year we'd doubled the size of the place, and annual volume went from $135,000 to $450,000."

KFC #2—The Sugarhouse Restaurant

In November 1953, Pete purchased a second restaurant, this time in the Salt Lake City suburb of Sugarhouse. The 225-seat Golden Flame became the second Harman Café, but was better known by employees as Sugarhouse.

"I was contacted by a wealthy local gentleman who owned the beautiful Golden Flame Restaurant in Sugarhouse, but it was losing $6,000 a month.

"When we talked it over, the wealthy gentleman said, 'Pay me what you want, over any time period you want to pay for it.' I consulted with my attorney and asked him to come up with a fair price for the property, which he did. Once I had that figure, I paid the original owner and took over my second restaurant. Then I set out to make it my own."

The remodeling included two neon signs. The first featured the words "Harman Café" in bold letters. The second featured the words "Kentucky Fried Chicken" standing high above the roof. Although the Golden Flame had not been profitable, Harman retained both the restaurant's original (and extensive) menu and employees.

At the end of the first month, he totaled the receipts. The restaurant lost $1,500. Pete said he was "shattered." He closed the restaurant early that day.

Harman desperately tried to figure out how to make the new restaurant profitable, eventually cutting the work force in half and reducing the menu offerings to a minimum. He also decided to

> *"You've got to put a lot of effort in whatever you do—you earn what you get."*
> —Pete Harman

experiment with a take-home department, managed by an enthusiastic former busboy named Einar Bergstedt. Within a few months, the new Harman Café showed a small profit.

Lesson learned: Large menus and staffs did not necessarily produce larger profits.

As business continued to expand in the weeks that followed, Pete and Arline needed more help. When he left for his annual trip to the NRA convention in May 1953, Harman left instructions with Ethel Parker, his assistant manager, to hire another carhop.

Jackie Joins the Team

Parker immediately contacted her niece, Jackie Trujillo (née Bills), an industrious high-school graduate from Logan in northern Utah. Trujillo had worked as a carhop since age fifteen and was looking for a summer job to earn enough money to attend college.

Harman returned two weeks later. He and Arline had gone on to Detroit following the convention and returned home in a yellow Cadillac DeVille. Upon his arrival, another employee, Mariam Gutke Holmes, stopped Harman and said, "This is Jackie, Ethel's niece." Harman nodded and said, "Oh, I'm glad to meet you," and went on. It was a low-key beginning for what would become a legendary partnership.

As fall approached, Trujillo made plans to attend Utah State University in Logan. "At the end of August, I had saved $350," Trujillo said. "I made sixty-five cents an hour when I started, but I made tips, too. In those days, if you made four or five dollars a day, you were doing pretty well.

"But my brother, who had four or five kids at the time, was in need of some financial help. So I said, 'Here, take this $350, and I'll keep working and earn enough money to go to college later.' I guess I never earned enough." And she never left Harman's.

Trujillo's Take on Pete

- ► Pete is the kind of guy who makes people feel special.
- ► He established a fun and creative atmosphere.
- ► He was a friendly presence in the restaurant, greeting and seating customers.
- ► Customer loyalty and marketing expertise resulted in sales increases each year.

Harman initially asked Trujillo to go to Sugarhouse as a cook, but Alice Hardy, the general manager, knew she could find more cooks. What she needed was a manager. "I was only eighteen years old," Trujillo said. "At that time, he didn't have really young people in managerial positions. They just didn't think that younger people were mature enough. But Alice offered me an opportunity to be an assistant manager, so she told Pete I was nineteen."

It wasn't long before his two restaurants were selling more chicken than their supplier could provide. So Pete went into the distribution business as well.

"He formed Quality Distribution Corporation," Trujillo recalls. "He came up to me one night at work and said he was going to sell stock in Quality. He offered me five hundred shares for five hundred dollars, and when I asked him where he thought I was going to get that

> "I had opportunities, so I've always wanted to share that with everyone else as well. I want people to work to have ownership. Quality is still a private corporation owned by the employees."
> —Pete Harman

kind of money, he loaned me the money to buy it. When I said, this better be a good deal, he just smiled and said, 'Don't worry about it.'"

Recruiting for KFC

It was a meeting of food-service greats, although neither man knew it at the time. Dave Thomas (of future Wendy's fame) was approached in his Indiana restaurant by a character who claimed to be an expert on fried chicken. "Who are you with, sir?" Dave asked the Colonel. The Colonel pounced on the opening.

Unlike most restaurant owners the Colonel solicited in those days, Thomas was convinced by his spiel and quickly added Kentucky Fried Chicken to his restaurant's menu.

Still, converts were few for the Colonel in the early days, although he remained undeterred and convinced that he offered a unique key to their success. Spreading the word was a daunting task, a test for the Colonel's physical and financial endurance.

Margaret Sanders said that her father would drive into towns where he'd had an inquiry on the night before an appointment. He would pick a well-lighted service station with a clean restroom, introduce himself to the owner, get permission to park and sleep in his car there overnight, and ask to hold the restroom key for his early morning routine. When he had shaved and changed into a freshly pressed suit that he kept hanging in his car, Father presented himself the next day as a successful franchisor to his prospective franchisee.

"In those days, we were just grateful that any restaurant owner had enough faith in us to use our recipe and cooking method. Father taught them how to cut a chicken into nine pieces so they could get three dinners out of one chicken."

In time, the Colonel's tireless promotion began to pay off as more and more restaurants finally began adding Kentucky Fried Chicken.

The Franchise Package

➤ The Colonel will visit your restaurant and instruct your staff on preparation and serving his chicken.

➤ He will supply at cost any cooking equipment you need, special spices packed for uniform quality, menu clipons, table tents, and place mats.

➤ The Colonel will gladly aid you in merchandising his chicken.

➤ You pay only a small royalty per order. That's right. You pay nothing above cost until you sell his chicken and profit from it.

In 1955, the Colonel boldly placed a full-page advertisement in *American Restaurant Magazine* with his franchise package offer. And beaming from the middle of this Kentucky Fried Chicken ad is the first national photograph of Colonel Sanders, resplendent in his black string tie and trademark white goatee and mustache.

Under a bold headline stating "Sales up 500%," a quote from Pete Harman reads, "In dollar terms—from $160,000 to $804,000 in three years with chicken doing 60%." It also is noted that Harman was receiving 8,300 orders a week for fried chicken. At the bottom of the advertisement is an invitation for prospective franchisees to contact either the Colonel himself or one of eight early franchise-holders:

Pete Harman, Salt Lake City
H.A. Harry, Breeseway Restaurant, Davenport, Iowa
Ted Cullen, Bluebird Restaurant, Morristown, Indiana
Carl Kaelin, Kaelin's Restaurant, Louisville, Kentucky
George Yonko, The Chuck Wagon, Gary, Indiana
Edward Clark, Robert E. Lee Motel, Bristol, Virginia
Eldred Dresden, Triangle Drive-In, Dixon, Illinois
Henry Boxman, Boxman's, Bloomington, Indiana

The Colonel Shifts Gears

After years of the Colonel's juggling his popular restaurant and his slowly emerging franchise business, fate intervened and forced a change of direction. The Eisenhower administration's campaign to connect the United States with a new interstate highway system had begun in earnest, and it became one of the great achievements of the twentieth century. But for the Colonel it was a disaster in the making. He was horrified to discover that the new "interstate" would bypass Corbin—and his popular restaurant and motel. Within a year after its construction, business had fallen 50 percent despite the restaurant's stellar reputation.

> *"Now I was sixty-five years old. I had my Social Security check to live on. But that was about all, and that wasn't very much. What was I to do? If I ever needed help from God, I needed it now."*
>
> —Harland Sanders

In 1956, the Colonel was forced to sell his beloved restaurant on public auction for $70,000—less than half of what he had been offered just a couple of years earlier. The sale barely covered taxes and outstanding bills.

While taking stock of his assets, the Colonel saw that his $105 Social Security check simply wouldn't stretch far enough each month to cover expenses. Suddenly, the idea of franchising his recipe had grown from being a lark and an excuse to scratch his itch for travel to more than a fallback position. With the loss of the restaurant, it suddenly became his last, best hope.

"I remember prayin' to God Almighty, 'You've helped me in the past, and I need your help now, God. And I promise you, if this idea of franchising works out because of your blessing, you'll get your share.'" It wasn't, Colonel Sanders admitted later, a very fancy-sounding prayer, but it was honest.

As he'd done many times in the past, the Colonel took off to do what he knew best—sell something. And, as before, his gifts as a salesman became his family's sole source of income.

He didn't know it at the time, but he had been thrust on a path toward undreamed of success. He had the product, and he had the talent to sell it.

Action on the Western Front

Fueled by non-stop advertising, soaring sales of Kentucky Fried Chicken, and the efforts of a dedicated staff, the Harmans decided to open another restaurant, choosing an existing establishment on North Temple Street in Salt Lake City in 1957. The "Harman Café" sign went up

> *The North Temple restaurant was designed with a take-home area at the back of the restaurant, as opposed to having one tacked on later. It proved to be immediately successful.*

with a slightly smaller sign that said, "Featuring Colonel Sanders Recipe Kentucky Fried Chicken" right beneath it. This was the first time the Colonel's "white-coat image" had been used in outdoor advertising.

It was clear to Pete Harman that something was happening with America's dining habits and that the take-home concept was somehow involved. Once again he was ahead of the curve, on the cutting edge of food-service strategy.

By 1957, the changes in America's tastes were widespread and becoming ingrained in the culture. The postwar boom had brought widespread affluence to large segments of the country. More and more families were using their newfound disposable income to buy television sets as well as other appliances. Eating out, once reserved for special occasions, became a regular occurrence as incomes increased. Television replaced motion pictures as the entertainment of choice, and families increasingly stayed home to watch popular programs such as *You Bet Your Life, Your Hit Parade, The $64,000 Question, Leave It to Beaver,* and *The Real McCoys.*

Pete shrewdly decided to seek more television coverage for Harman-North Temple. On opening day, the two local television stations broadcast live from the restaurant. A still photo from the opening on March 31, 1957, shows Pete and Arline smiling proudly in front of a spray of chrysanthemums.

"They had two cameras," Harman recalled, "one in the dining room where they introduced our management team and one camera downstairs to show the parking garage. Then they moved the upstairs camera to the kitchen, where they made an eighty-gallon soup pot look like a tanker."

Harman-North Temple was a handsome two-story restaurant with a coffee shop in front, underground parking, and an upstairs dining hall for when existing seating couldn't handle the crowds. That brought the seating total to three hundred. And, as with the Golden Flame, Harman's marketing savvy soon turned North Temple into a money-making enterprise.

Among those employees who *didn't* make the trip to Harman-North Temple was Jackie Trujillo. By now, Harman was leaning heavily on the young woman, who was proving to be a quick study in the restaurant business.

> *"When you were part of management at Harman's, you automatically were a team player. Just as Pete always said that he wanted to succeed for his Aunt Carrie, we all wanted to succeed for him."*
>
> —Jackie Trujillo

Jackie's role was to be a trouble-shooter for the Harmans, moving from one of their establishments to another as the need arose. "If that was where he needed me, then that's what I did. I don't remember even thinking twice about it. That's the benefit of having a boss who made you a part of the process."

Buoyed by the success of his restaurants, Harman responded not by hoarding money and building a private fortune, but by looking to reward employees who were the foundation of his success.

//////

Pete's Words of Wisdom

▶ Employees want to work for a fair employer, and if you will give them a halfway decent break, they'll go a long way beyond the capacity they think they've got.

▶ We don't look for anything special when hiring people—the cream usually rises to the top on its own.

▶ We believe in motivating, educating, and celebrating people.

▶ Every executive in our company started out frying chicken or working at the front counter. We've grown from within—and I'll put our organization up against any company in America for efficiency.

▶ Don't fire the cook on Friday night.

▶ Money is only as good as the good you do with it.

"We had three big restaurants in Utah, and they were really booming," Harman recalls thinking at the time. I sat down in a booth one day and two of the greatest ladies in the world were waiting on tables there, and I thought, 'These gals are forty years old. What are they going to do when they reach sixty? They won't be able to work at this pace.'"

"So I decided that every employee in the company would receive a contribution of the same amount. Over the years, the plan has performed well and has benefited everyone equally.

"There is a mentally challenged young man in Utah who now has over $500,000 in his pension fund. His dad brought him in and wanted to know if he could wash dishes. He broke half the dishes he washed in the early days, but he's got more than a half a million bucks in the fund now. The investments are a key. I don't know how much money is in our profit-sharing plan or our retirement fund, but it's a lot."

Profit sharing was not common in American business in the late 1950s. So where did Harman come up with the concept?

Perhaps it was Aunt Carrie's generous nature. Perhaps he heard something at the annual National Restaurant Association conventions he attended religiously. Harman himself no longer remembers the origins of the concept.

But Jackie Trujillo believes the idea was a logical outgrowth of Harman's worldview. "Pete focused on two areas. The first was to grow the business because he knew that we had to do that in order to make more opportunities for people and to keep building new stores.

> *"Pete's most significant contribution to the restaurant industry is to teach us. He taught us that you could grow a business as long as you allowed the people who were making the money for you to share in the fruits of their labor. He has taught this industry how to make a manager/ownership program work."*
> —Don Smith

"He is always looking for ways to help his employees," said Barrie McKay, longtime lawyer for the Harmans. "Back in June 1957, he pulled a rabbit out of the hat. He wanted the employees to share in the profits. He thought that they ought to. So he asked us to put together a profit-sharing plan—long before it was conceived of by most people. He put together a plan where all employees shared equally regardless of their position or salary. And that is the only one that I know of in the country today that still does that. The janitor gets the same amount in profit-sharing that Pete Harman does."

Don Smith, a motivational speaker and a professor from the University of Washington's School of Restaurant Management, said that Harman's generous nature was actually good business. And Jackie Trujillo said, "His heart's desire was to help people build a career that had both prestige and offered them a good lifestyle. He wanted them to have something that would enable them to maintain that same lifestyle in their old age. He was obsessed with seeing that everybody was well taken care of as they got older."

Harman's plan was important to new employees like Shirley Hamblin: "When I started at Harman Café on August 3,

1957, I had been divorced, had five children, and no means of support. I think the second night I worked on the floor is when I met Pete. He came up, and I thought he was the janitor. Then I found out who he was. Pete has just been so wonderful to my family. I know he always worried that I wasn't going to make enough money. He knew how many children I had, and he wanted to make sure that I could make a living for them.

> *Pete Harman found that empowering, praising, and rewarding his employees produced superior results. He codified the core assumptions that underpinned every personnel move he made. Eventually, they were written down and placed in conspicuous places throughout his restaurants—where they remain even today.*

The first Thanksgiving I worked for him he made sure that Betty Allen gave me twenty dollars for a turkey and food for the family. He was always like that."

Working With Women

If America was experiencing a postwar boom, American working women were seeing precious little of it. Not all jobs were open to them, and while nursing and teaching positions were chronically underpaid, at least there were some benefits. For the vast majority of secretaries and waitresses, there was little hope of advancement and virtually no supplemental benefits.

Not so at Harman Cafés. In fact, in addition to the profit-sharing plan, Pete was a pioneer in actively promoting women into management positions. "Right after World War II, you *had* to hire women," Harman said. "All the guys could go to college for nothing on the GI Bill, and it's right after that we really took off. Women are loyal. They're good business people. I didn't hire and promote them out of sympathy—I needed them."

Trujillo recalls that, "When I first started in the business, we only had women mangers, there were no men managers. Pete hired all women. I think he loved working with women, but he cared because of who you were and the talent you had.

You could see that. He could look at somebody and say, 'Boy, they really need this opportunity—they don't have anything. How can I get them into a management position so that they can earn enough money to take care of their family?'"

From the beginning, Harman put women in charge of every facet of his restaurants. Only the grill and chicken cooks were predominantly men.

"Mainly everybody out front was a woman," he said. "Every manager was a woman. One of the reasons was because you couldn't support a larger family (on a single salary). That was the reason the women were working anyway, because they had to have a supplement to their husband's job."

How many women? A photograph of Harman employees from 1958 features nineteen women and only two men. Significantly—in spite of the Jim Crow segregation days of the late 1950s—it also includes one African-American, Adell Rogers.

Shirley Hamblin maintained that for Harman there are no unimportant jobs. "One thing that Pete loves to do is walk in a store, go back in the cook room, and say to the cook, 'I'm Pete Harman, how are you doing? Is everybody treating you okay? Is everything going okay? Do you like your job?' I think Pete would love it if all of us would carry on those same traditions and always remember to recognize the people in our crews. Because a lot of us don't take the time—we get so busy that we forget that cook, (and) that's where most of us started out."

After more than thirty years with Harman, Hazel Fong— today regional director for the far-flung San Francisco/East Bay Region—was even more direct about how all employees, including women, were compensated the same:

"I got paid the same amount as a man for doing the same job. Pete has always done this with women because, as he always says, 'It was just the right thing to do.'"

"Even today, women typically only get paid 70 percent of what men get paid for the same job, but not at Harman's," Trujillo said. "We've never had a discrimination lawsuit, because Pete has always insisted that equal work gets equal pay. And he did it from the beginning—long before it was required by law. That's just Pete."

Obviously, Harman's trust in women managers eventually reaped huge dividends. One of his favorite stories involves long-time manager Alice Hardy. She eventually oversaw all of Harman's Utah-based restaurants and inspired fierce loyalty among her vendors.

"She was the chief purchasing agent, and boy—you talk about loyalty for suppliers," Harman said. "Lots of times there would be shortages for two or three products. I'd call her up and say, 'Alice, how are you going to make out?' And just then a supplier would phone her up and say, 'Don't you worry, Alice. You'll get your supplies.' And she always did.

"That's the history of our company. Every executive started frying chicken or waiting on customers at the front counter. We've grown from within. And I'll put our organization up to any company in America for results."

Pete and the Colonel in front of the Sugarhouse restaurant,
Harman's second KFC restaurant

The Birth of the Bucket—and More

The gradual expansion of KFC from one franchisee to dozens, then eventually hundreds, paralleled a great change in America's dining habits. With the advent of the first bucket, Harman gifted KFC with an enduring icon that would enable customers to enjoy "Sunday dinner seven days a week"—a valuable asset in the age of the automobile.

But the bucket emerged only because someone was paying close attention to *every* aspect of the restaurant business. There are no unimportant factors in the complex process of delivering high quality food to hungry consumers—and doing so profitably.

What Pete and the Colonel learned and trumpeted was a secret that has inspired countless entrepreneurs and corporations alike in the years that followed:

Success is in the details—every penny counts.

Pete's fertile imagination and persistence in exploring possibilities for his restaurants were perpetually at work during the early days of expansion. In 1957, he wrestled in the back of his mind with an idea that was tantalizing with possibilities, but packaging solutions were elusive.

> *A smoothly running machine requires all cogs and pieces working in perfect tandem. And it takes every component of a business working in sync to produce a quality product every time—while putting money in the bank.*
> —KFC philosophy

He always kept his eye on the competition, including Beau Brummel's, one of the nicest restaurants in Salt Lake City. It was offering a prime rib dinner for $3.50 and doing very well with it. Pete wanted to surpass that enticement, and he finally came up with the idea of serving a family of five for $3.50. How to pull it off was a problem.

Someone else's mistake provided the answer and changed how the world ate chicken forever.

"This gentleman in Greeley, Colorado, had purchased five hundred buckets for his restaurant, but didn't know what to do with them," Pete recalled later. "The Colonel called and wanted to know if we would take them off his hands."

Jackie Trujillo remembers the day Pete came into the restaurant with the first bucket and said, "We need to sell larger orders to build the business. Let's put fourteen pieces in this bucket and make it a new menu item that will feed a family of five. In order to build our business, we need to sell larger orders."

At the time, the Harman restaurants were offering a dinner box with three pieces of chicken in it.

> *"The choice of fourteen pieces is still something of a mystery. But Pete probably had it all figured out that this was how to hold the price to $3.50."*
> —Jackie Trujillo

Pete wanted to offer five rolls with the new dinner and to improve the bucket's heft at the same time. Even with the rolls added, he wasn't happy with how it felt. "This doesn't weigh enough. It doesn't feel like $3.50." So he dumped the chicken out and stuck a pint of gravy in the bottom then put the chicken around it.

"What if they dump this thing out and the gravy spills?" Pete was asked. "Oh hell, they'll figure it out. But now it feels like $3.50," he responded.

The advent of the bucket brought about a significant transformation in Pete's restaurants. It was decided to strictly limit what was available through the take-out sections and rely almost solely on the bucket.

Pete and his team had known for some time that they had to get down to a more simplified menu or they weren't going to be able to wait on customers fast enough.

"We decided that if they wanted to come in the restaurant and sit down, they could have anything they wanted," Trujillo recalls. "If they wanted to come through the take-home department, we simplified the menu. The first thing we took off was hamburgers. Yes, we might have lost some customers, but if you sold one bucket of chicken, that would have been the equivalent of seventeen and a half hamburgers."

> *"It didn't take us long to realize that with that one bucket, our service was going to be better. We had to get faster, we had to get more convenient, and we had to trim our menu."*
> —Jackie Trujillo

Harman was so certain he had a winner with the buckets that he asked Alan Frank, who played a major role in advertising, to design and print 125 miniature billboard sheets—enough to blanket the county—touting his $3.50 meal deal. "He asked me to get hold of a billboard company," Frank recalled. "They used to have what we called miniature billboards, and Pete was sure they had empty spaces all over the city. He said he'd pay for the paper until they could sell the rest of them.

The Harman restaurants sold out their first order of buckets in a few days, which caused a scramble to find more. The advertising campaign began on Monday, and it soon became obvious that they would run out by the weekend. Somehow Pete scrounged up another two hundred buckets, and it was Saturday before he located more of them in Los Angeles and had them flown in.

"By Saturday, we'd tracked down a gentleman with Lynn Wilson Salads," Trujillo said. "Pete asked if he had any extra buckets—and he did. That filled the void for a time. But these had been intended for the storage of cold products and were lined with wax. In desperation, we turned the buckets upside down on a cookie sheet and placed them in the ovens. The heat melted the wax off.

> *When you try something, put 120 percent in it. If it doesn't work, forget that sucker. Then do something else. Don't stew over it. If it doesn't work, it doesn't work.*
>
> —Pete Harman

"When we ran out of those, Pete's old Sunday School teacher knew about an Army plane that flew regularly to L.A. for Sears & Roebuck. It had some space, and Pete ordered a ton of buckets for the return run. By the weekend, we had the buckets we needed. And we've never run out of buckets since!"

The bucket enabled a family to eat together at home—and watch their favorite television shows. It also enabled harried mothers to provide a nutritious meal without spending hours in the kitchen. And in Mormon Utah, where large families are the norm, the bucket was an instant hit—and remains popular decades later.

"Sunday Dinner, Seven Days a Week"

Sundays were the biggest day of the week for Pete's bucket business, and keeping up with it was a pleasant problem. It was quickly discovered that the bucket had another advantage—it also was great for Sunday picnics, a popular pastime for Americans in those days. It wasn't long before every trip to the beach, the mountains, or the back yard was accompanied by a bucket of KFC chicken.

Soon, every bucket that accompanied a family on a weekend getaway as well as in their homes was a spokesman for the chicken it contained. The next generation of buckets was printed in red and white with the Kentucky Fried Chicken logo and the Colonel's face on it—making the bucket itself a physical advertisement that would, in time, become a national icon.

Pete had another brainstorm. He wanted to get involved in the community, so he developed the idea of the bucket of chicken as a fundraiser. He told different organizations, "If you go out and sell these buckets of chicken, you can make a dollar or dollar and a half on every one you sell. So the Scouts, for example, would go door-to-door, take the orders, and would come in and request fifty or one hundred buckets in a single evening. Of course, we'd get all this chicken ready for the Scouts to pick it up and deliver it."

The story of Harman's success with the bucket concept spread to the other early Kentucky Fried Chicken franchisees and they, too—save probably for a franchisee in Greeley, Colorado— began ordering and promoting their own buckets.

> *"We did a lot of advertising, with 125 billboards, radio advertising, and a little bit of television. We could hardly pack them fast enough—and there were only three restaurants. It was a huge market that had never been tapped."*
>
> —Pete Harman

Not that the bucket was perfect. Harman wasn't satisfied with the original version of the bucket, which had an inside ring that was supposed to help seal the container. Harman said less than one in ten buckets actually worked that way. It took a friend's candid comments to address the bucket's major design flaw.

"In 1958, Jim Durbin was the manager of the Hotel Utah," Harman said. "He invited us to join his family at a resort where we could relax and fish. We grabbed a couple of buckets of chicken and went up to the resort. But when we opened the buckets, there was so much moisture that the rolls and everything inside the buckets was soggy like you wouldn't believe. So we got an ice pick and punched a bunch of holes in the lids. Then it worked fine. We had our managers punch holes in the lids until the next revised order of lids—with holes in them— finally arrived."

Word of Pete's success with Kentucky Fried Chicken spread not just across Utah but also among his far-flung family. He made it a family affair later that year when his brother

Jack Harman opened Harman's Restaurant in Yakima, Washington, with the now-familiar "Kentucky Fried Chicken" logo.

Pete's brother Dave Harman also opened a large restaurant that featured Kentucky Fried Chicken in Phoenix. And it is Dave who was partly responsible for coining one of the most enduring phrases in the history of American advertising: "It's finger-lickin' good!"

Dave had commercials in the afternoon between the movies they used to show in the old days of television. But in time he had a stroke and couldn't talk, so his manager, Ken Harbough, did the commercials. But Dave still wanted to be in show business, so he would take a plate of chicken down to the station and eat it in the background during the filming of the commercial.

"One day, a woman phoned up—just mad as the devil— and said, 'That Mr. Harman is licking his fingers!' Ken spontaneously said, 'Well, it's finger lickin' good!' And that was our slogan for years and years," Pete recalled.

The Colonel Makes a Move

Meanwhile, with the loss of his restaurant, the Colonel was casting about for a new location for his fledgling franchising business. Daughter Mildred Ruggles recalled that he wanted a location that would make it easier to ship products to his franchisees.

"Eventually, with the road bypassing Corbin, Daddy realized it was time he had to move on. One day we were going out the old Shelbyville Road towards Louisville and I said, 'Daddy, there's a house for sale.' It was a big old house. He said, 'Daughter, when we come back, we'll stop and go in.' So we did and he bought it. He called up Claudia and said, 'We're moving to Shelbyville. I just bought a house.' That got him up to where he could get into shipping. This was very important because at this time the franchisees were getting larger in number. The word was really out about the chicken."

Now operating out of a white brick house in Shelbyville, the Colonel continued his relentless crusade, preaching the gospel of Kentucky Fried Chicken. An early convert was the Hobby House Restaurant in Fort Wayne, Indiana. Among the thousands who ate the Original Recipe was Kenny King, a restaurant operator from Cleveland. King raved about the chicken when he got back home.

> *"I needed to be near a big town, but I didn't want to live in one. This let me live in a small town and still be only twenty-five miles from Louisville."*
> —Harland Sanders

Later, the owner of the Hobby House passed through Cleveland and stopped at the King family's restaurant for a visit. He mentioned that he needed to get back to Fort Wayne for the busy season.

"My father's ears perked up at that remark," Kenny King Jr. recalled, "because in the hamburger business in Cleveland you're not busy in January and February. He told him that Kentucky Fried Chicken made the difference. So we went looking for the Colonel and became franchisees in 1959."

The Colonel was a human dynamo. He left people half his age struggling to keep up. At nine or ten at night, after a day and a half of hard work, he'd say good night, adding, 'I'll see you at six.' But eventually, with new restaurants signing up on a regular basis, even someone with the Colonel's bull-like constitution couldn't be everywhere at once, so he began to assemble a team to help him operate his new Kentucky Fried Chicken Corporation.

An early hiree was Lee Cummings, a native of Henryville, Indiana, and the son of the Colonel's sister Catherine. Cummings had worked for the Colonel at Sanders Court and Motel in Corbin before becoming a bread salesman. In February 1958, he rejoined the Colonel as Kentucky Fried Chicken's first vice-president.

Cummings was originally hired to handle inquiries, make kitchen layouts for new franchise holders, and train franchise holders in "the true art of cooking Kentucky Fried Chicken." But Cummings quickly found that he had other—originally unspecified—duties as well.

Once, when money was scarce in the early days, a Chicago restaurant supplier owed the Colonel $1,300 on an equipment package. Cummings said that the supplier refused to pay even when the Colonel sent a field representative to collect in person. The rep called the Colonel from the supplier's office and handed him the phone. "The rep said the guy got so outraged at whatever the Colonel was saying to him that he ripped his own phone off the wall and turned over his own desk," Cummings recalled. "As he proceeded to wreck his own office, the rep ran out.

"A week later, the Colonel and I drove to Chicago to collect the debt," Cummings remembered. "We secretly cased the joint one evening—in the white Cadillac with the Colonel's mug on both doors. The next morning, when the man and his son-in-law opened up, we followed them right into their office before they spotted us. They were startled when they saw us. Then the Colonel laid out that invoice and said, 'I came to collect my damn money!'

"The older man said, 'You wouldn't call a man to his face what you called me on the phone, would you?'

"'Yes, I would, and in case you have forgotten what I said—' and the Colonel gave him both barrels again. The guy was shaking so bad after that that his son-in-law had to work the combination of the safe to get out the checkbook, and had to write the check. We took it to the nearest bank, cashed it and were on our way back to Kentucky when the Colonel said, 'I guess those city fellers thought they could cheat a mountain man.'"

Pete the Motivator

Even during the lean early days of the Do Drop Inn, Pete Harman was endlessly creative in devising new incentives for his staff. One was a simple pool: each staff member put a quarter in the kitty and guessed the day's total receipts. The person who came closest to the actual amount in the till got to keep the pot.

As his total number of restaurants grew, Harman cast
about for new incentives and
ways to reward loyal, productive
employees. Perhaps it was the
success of that early lottery that
convinced Pete to take his managers on Harman's first incentive
vacation to Las Vegas in 1958.

> *"When you hire somebody, probably the greatest thing you can do is make them believe they are going to be successful. The second key is to let them know you care."*
>
> —Pete Harman

"The first trip was very small," Harman said, "we only had a few restaurants. It was designed to achieve harmony and keep jealousies out of the way. We had two families that were jealous of one another, so we got in two cars. We also said that no man and wife could sit together. At every stop to gas up, we changed cars, moved them around. We went down to the El Rancho, and it was the first year that they had gambling. We stayed one night, got in the cars and came back. Those couples worked together just fine after that."

The Harman Empire Expands

On November 4, 1959, Pete opened Harman's Original Pancake House in the Salt Lake suburb of Murray, with the words "Pancakes of Every Nationality" emblazoned across the roof. Harman said the idea for a pancake house came during a trip to California.

"The International Pancake House started up in Oregon, and we got a franchise for it," he said. "We visited one in San Mateo, and they had waiting lines you couldn't believe. So we opened one on 50th South and State Street, and it was an immediate hit. On Saturday and Sunday mornings people waited in line to get in the doors."

Although Harman's Original Pancake House lasted only another four years, it was particularly popular with Pete and Arline's son Barry. Once again, Harman sensed a promotional opportunity. "The twenty-fourth of July celebrates the Mormon arrival in Salt Lake Valley and always is celebrated across the state with parades. One year, when Barry was maybe sixteen or seventeen, all the kids his age were on a float. They got some steel wool, put some pancake batter in it, shaped it like pancakes, then cooked a number of them so they would be solid. They flipped pancakes for eighteen blocks. The *Deseret News* had that on the front page."

Pete's Words of Wisdom

▶ Everybody's success in business in this: You're only as successful as your people are going to be.
▶ The philosophy of our company is to make the store managers successful by treating them as partners.
▶ Be around your people a lot. Let them know daily how you feel. And teach the managers to do the same.

Harman's first venture out of greater Salt Lake City came with the opening of another Harman Café, this time in Ogden, about thirty-five miles north. Like the others, it did well from the beginning. The Colonel himself was at the grand opening on November 20, 1959, and a full-page ad from that date claims that he gave "ladies a recipe book from his famous collection of favorite southern dishes."

This wasn't just Pete's café. Lester H. and Ileene Rufer were spotlighted as co-managers, a first for the Harman company. Lester had been head chef at Harman's North Temple restaurant, while Ileene was the past manager of Harman's Sugarhouse Café. The ad stated that the couple moved to Ogden to operate the new restaurant, Harman's Millstream

Road. Harman offered the Rufers 40 percent stock ownership to assume control of the new place.

According to Barrie McKay, Harman's long-time lawyer, once Pete began to expand his chain of restaurants systematically, he always treated the storeowners as partners. "He said, 'This is my partner; come and meet my partner,'" and they were the owners. He always felt that if they had an ownership, they would take more pride, they will take more responsibility, and they also would get more benefits."

Pete now had five restaurants. Every day he would be at four of them—he'd go to breakfast at one, lunch at another, dinner at still another, and visit the last one in the afternoon. He knew all those customers and they knew that Pete Harman was the owner.

When he put the fifth restaurant thirty-five miles north of Salt Lake City, he said, "I am not going to be able to be there every day, so I need to get a partner. The customers who patronize the business need to know who the owner is. And if they are going to do all the work, then they need to have some ownership."

Les had a lot of experience in the restaurant business. He was a chef; he knew a lot about food and recipes, and he was efficient with cost control. He was very successful. And with the addition of the first restaurant outside of Salt Lake City, Harman began to emphasize a friendly rivalry among his restaurants.

"We wanted to beat one another," Jackie Trujillo said. "We have always been that way. We are a very competitive company, even though we are the world's greatest team. We live and survive on measurements, and Pete had a lot of ways of measuring results—still does today.

"Les and Ileene soon ran better numbers than we were. We teased Les, accusing him of cheating. He was the first man we had running a business, so some of the women got a little jealous. We found out later that he was succeeding because he had created a lot of his own menu items. He could run better food costs because he had more experience in creating the actual menu. We improved our costs, too—we learned some things from the Rufers."

And Kentucky Fried Chicken remained the best-selling item on the menu.

"That was the last full-service restaurant we built," Trujillo said. In the days that followed, Harman studied the bottom line at each restaurant and eventually reached a radical conclusion. There was a more economical way to meet the customers' needs and offer even more growth in management and ownership.

He knew what he wanted to do, but he wasn't quite ready to take the plunge and devote a restaurant exclusively to a take-home business featuring Kentucky Fried Chicken. That move came from another direction.

Chicken-to-Go

Working independently, someone else had come to the same conclusion and did something about it—the Colonel's daughter Margaret. She always had successfully resisted her father's efforts to involve her in the restaurant business in the past. But during a trip from her home in Coconut Grove to Shelbyville, Margaret Sanders devised a compromise solution:

"The thought occurred to me that it would be a great idea if we had a place where we would cook Father's Original Recipe chicken, and people could take it out in boxes to the beach or wherever they chose to eat it. By the time I reached Kentucky, I had formulated how I was going to approach Father with my 'Nothing-But-Chicken-to-Go' idea.

"I realized I would be talking about a concept that was a far cry from the restaurant business to which Father had been so accustomed. He already knew he couldn't get me into the kitchen to cook, so my game plan had to be carefully laid out in a way that Father could accept. I had to start by emphasizing the difference between a restaurant where all kinds of foods were being cooked as opposed to a place where they would come specifically to pick up boxed chicken to take with them."

When she finally met with the Colonel, Margaret said a quick prayer, then launched into her carefully rehearsed spiel— adding that the casual dress code made Florida a logical testing ground for the new concept. According to Margaret, her father was dubious at first about the plan's prospects.

"After his response, I waited a bit and gathered my thoughts, then reminded him that I played an important role in the whole scheme of things. I began to plead my case, 'Father, you remember that you used me as your chief taste-tester while you were experimenting with all those herbs and spices trying to find the perfect combination.'"

In time, the Colonel confessed that take-out was, indeed, an idea whose time had come. In February 1958, on Margaret's forty-seventh birthday, he gave her exclusive rights to Kentucky Fried Chicken in Florida and, later that year, the first stand-alone take-away was built.

The Colonel soon saw that the future lay with "stand-alone" franchises: "She (Margaret) said, if she just had a place that cooked Kentucky Fried Chicken, where the people would come and take it home, she would like that. And that's what gave us the idea of the freestandin' 'take-home' store that has really put Kentucky Fried Chicken on the map."

While Margaret had her way in Florida, Barney's Restaurant in Calgary, Canada offered what is believed to be among the first home delivery in modern fast-food history. Consumers could order any amount of Kentucky Fried Chicken by dialing CHI-CKEN.

> *"I accepted it as the way of the future. I thought we gave better value and better service this way. It was a lot easier on everyone. And it was more fun!"*
> —Jackie Trujillo

It was an instant hit, although other franchisees were slow to add home delivery to their stores.

Not surprisingly, what was working in Florida and Calgary also worked in Utah. After opening the full-service restaurant in Ogden, Harman went exclusively to stand-alone, take-home restaurants featuring Kentucky Fried Chicken.

"By the time we got to ten take-home restaurants, we knew that they were the future," Trujillo said. "They were much easier to run and the labor costs were so much lower. Full-service restaurants simply cost so much more to run.

Plus, you have to keep remodeling them every few years. It made more sense to have less overhead, less square footage, and generate more income."

A second determining factor, she said, was that full-service restaurants needed more property and cost considerably more to build. A third factor was that it was a better return on investments for Harman and the co-partner or manager team to open and run a restaurant.

"These new owners/partners were often waitresses who had become managers and brought their husbands into the business," Trujillo said. "With take-home, they could run the business themselves with ten to twelve employees. You couldn't do that with a full-service restaurant. Nor did many of them have enough in the bank to build a restaurant from scratch."

Harman began converting his original five full-service restaurants into take-homes. The restaurant at 39th South was the last to convert in the 1970s. In 1960, Harman's-7th East & 3rd South Street became one of the first freestanding take-home restaurants in the country. It still featured the "Harman" name, but the Colonel's face and "Kentucky Fried Chicken" were more prominent.

In December of that year, Harman opened his second freestanding Kentucky Fried Chicken at 3310 South 23rd East Street in Salt Lake City.

Each of these new restaurants soon reinforced Pete's original suspicions: the take-home restaurants specializing in Kentucky Fried Chicken were making a better profit than the big, full-service restaurants. Profit was to be made from selling buckets of chicken at a low price, not from extensive, labor-intensive menus and large staffs.

Harman's First Trainer

But owning that many restaurants created other problems, including staffing. Harman soon realized that if his budding chain were to continue to grow, it would need some kind of uniform training for continuity's sake. He turned again to Jackie Bills

Trujillo. He had heard at a recent NRA convention that the national Bob's Big Boy restaurant chain had instituted a training program for its employees. Intrigued, he sent her to Los Angeles to learn all she could from the Bob's Big Boy program.

"He flew me down there and I went through their training process," Trujillo said. "It taught you, through slides and through a narrative, the way you do things and how important service is. Then you actually worked on the job with someone at that restaurant. I thought, 'This is fairly easy. I think I can do this.' So, on the way back home, I put the thing together— the plan, and the program, the agenda.

"When I got back, Pete said, 'What do you need?' I said, 'I need a photographer. Here is the layout.' When the photographer came, I said, 'Here are the slides I want you to take. Here is my model.' The photographer took the slides and, once I had them in sequence, that was all I needed. I then wrote the script. The next Saturday we were in business and had our first training meeting for the waitresses. And every new waitress from then on went through it."

Trujillo later created comparable training sessions for cooks as well. Harman attended her first session for waitresses, nodded his approval, and didn't return again to the Saturday morning sessions for several months.

"About eight months after the first training meeting, he came into my meeting again," Trujillo recalled. "I gave the same presentation, with the same enthusiasm that I'd had eight months earlier. I thought it was kind of funny that he was there.

"When I had finished the meeting, he said 'You really did good today. That was as good as the first meeting you gave.'

"Pete said, 'I am going to expand your job. I'm going to put you into a full-time training position, and I want you to go out to the restaurants and train people. We're growing, and training is an important key to our future success. And, oh yeah, we need to have a training manual,

> "When you are a dedicated trainer, never give up an opportunity to make a difference in a person's education. Every trainee is an opportunity for the future."
> —Jackie Trujillo

too. That means we've got to write down everything that has to be done within the restaurant and how it is done.'"

Trujillo promptly crafted Harman's first operations manual. "It was very timely and helped us with our future growth," she said. "It standardized our operations, procedures and management practices. It was confirmed and adopted by everyone in a management position, and I think it brought a greater consistency within our entire company."

Trujillo's detailed descriptions of important tasks and obligations included such gripping chapters as:

> "Waiting on Customers"
> "Maintenance of Equipment"
> "Sanitation"
> "Recipes and Procedures of Products"

Trujillo was then officially promoted from "Jackie-of-All-Trades" to Harman's First Trainer. And her first stab at a manual was adopted—almost verbatim—by Kentucky Fried Chicken's corporate offices in 1963.

Employees as Owners

▶ Empowerment creates loyalty and accountability.

▶ Empowerment plus thirst for excellence translate into success.

▶ Empowerment creates a climate where facilities sparkle.

▶ Empowerment produces first-rate customer service.

▶ Empowerment is created by a culture that recognizes and encourages the success of others.

5

Holding a Tiger by Its Tail

In time, KFC grew so fast that even the apparently untiring Colonel was forced to sell. But even the new owners recognized the foundations of the success of the brand. As Pete Harman and the Colonel had done before them, the new ownership systematically sought ways to empower those who worked for them. Empowerment creates loyalty, accountability, and a thirst for excellence that invariably translates into success. It creates a climate where facilities sparkle, first-rate customer service is a given, the product is presented with obvious care, and employees remain and flourish. Empowerment is created by a culture that recognizes and encourages the success of others.

That lesson—*Make employees owners in your business and they'll think and act like owners*—is still a revolutionary concept with most corporations. But where it has been embraced and blessed by management, it has created a fertile environment that breeds even more success. With today's KFC, it is the pervasive legacy of a handful of profoundly influential founders.

As the nation moved into the turbulent, unpredictable sixties, no corporate entity epitomized stability and steady growth more than Kentucky Fried Chicken. The Colonel's perpetual push for sales, constant travel, and nights sleeping in his car had paid off, and there was every reason to believe that his company's spectacular success would continue unabated.

> *"During most of his waking hours, the Colonel is haunted by the fear that someone, somewhere is doing something to hurt his chicken—that some upstart in the company is tampering with the recipe, or that a careless franchisee is undercooking or overcooking.*
> —The New Yorker
> February 14, 1970

More than two hundred restaurants in the United States and six in Canada were selling his Original Recipe at an amazing rate. Prospective franchisees now came in a steady stream to see the Colonel at his rambling home in Shelbyville, where he would serve massive breakfasts of country ham, red-eye gravy, and hot biscuits.

And by now the Colonel had perfected his trademark look—including white suits, string ties, and flowing white hair and beard—which he presented to the public at all times. He had become a national celebrity, making the rounds of radio and television talk shows, often demonstrating his prowess in the kitchen.

The franchising boom that was beginning to sweep the nation was continuing in Utah as well. Pete Harman now had eleven restaurants, an accounting office, a distribution center, and more than four hundred employees. Harman had sensed, just as had the Colonel, that the time was right to expand dramatically. Long stretches of commercially zoned property had suddenly opened in four counties in California as the postwar flight to the suburbs expanded; and those suburbs were populated mainly by young families in need of quick, wholesome, inexpensive dining choices. At the time, Harman was building one restaurant every twenty-eight days.

In 1964, the Colonel had seven hundred franchises, allocating many to friends and family members. Most were still sealed with a handshake or a rudimentary contract. The Colonel preferred to trust people, including his franchisees. And why not? The franchises were grossing more than $37 million a year.

But the Colonel's hardscrabble life and advancing age had begun to take its toll. In the days before franchising was widely accepted, the Colonel had admitted that each sale took a serious emotional and physical investment. Now there were the first rumblings of a possible change in ownership.

The Colonel had begun Kentucky Fried Chicken from scratch at age sixty-five, and in nine years he had built an empire. "The popularity of Kentucky Fried Chicken was growin' right over me and mashin' me flat. I just couldn't keep up with it," he said.

Shirley Topmiller, his personal secretary for many years, added, "He had a tiger by the tail. There were people calling every day. He still felt he needed to visit every franchisee. The house couldn't hold all of the people who were trying to buy franchises. And he was not a young man."

Enter John Y. Brown

It was at this point that John Y. Brown Jr. entered the Colonel's life. Others had approached the Colonel in the past to buy his chicken recipe and the concept, but he'd rebuffed all such efforts—until now.

Of John Y. Brown Jr., the Colonel once said, "With that oratory he's got, he could take a greasy pig and make it think it's on its way to Sunday School." The Colonel was well acquainted with both "young" John, the future governor of Kentucky, and his well-known father, John

> *"Colonel, you're seventy-four years old. You've developed a wonderful product in Kentucky Fried Chicken. And you've worked hard doing it, but now is the time for you to relax."*
> —Jack Massey

Y. Brown Sr., a former congressman from Kentucky, through

the restaurant and through the Colonel's occasional forays into politics.

> "You couldn't separate the Colonel from the chicken. He was not just the image. He was the company."
>
> —John Y. Brown

Brown had parlayed exceptional people skills and a charismatic presence into successful careers selling vacuum cleaners and encyclopedias while attending law school. He eventually declined a manager's position with Encyclopedia Britannica to open a modest law practice in Louisville. At the time, after moderating a televised debate, he received an unexpected call from old family friend Harland Sanders to discuss business possibilities.

"Around Kentucky then, we didn't know what the Colonel was up to," said Brown. "A lot of people thought he was sort of a hoax, walking around in a white suit and a mustache, driving a Cadillac with his mug shot on it. But he was a friend of my father, and trusted my father. They were from the old school.

"At that point in my career, when he called me, I decided that making money was what was really important if I wanted to do what I wanted to in my life—politics. I wasn't quite making $30,000 a year as a lawyer, even though back then that was a lot of money. But I knew I was really a salesman, not an attorney.

"Finally, in my second year of law practice, I decided that I needed to get into business. But I didn't know what business was. I'd never read a balance sheet. We didn't study anything like that in law school. I just played poker all the time and sold books. When the Colonel called me, it was the right time. I took off for six months to see if there was a fit."

Once the two finally met face-to-face, Brown was immediately intrigued. "He took me upstairs and showed me all the royalty checks, for $120, $200, and $380," Brown recalled. "And he had about six hundred of them. I said, 'My gosh, this thing is a real money maker.'"

The Colonel offered Brown a position handling the company's real estate acquisitions—something he knew nothing about. "He had six hundred franchisees, and when I asked him how many salesmen he used, he said, 'None. We just don't believe in solicitation.'"

The Colonel Speaks

➤ I feel that this food miracle, Kentucky Fried Chicken, may be my only contribution to the restaurant industry—that's the one reason I am so meticulous about the way it is prepared and the quality of it all.

➤ My determination to give my customers only the finest—and my years of experimenting with Kentucky Fried Chicken—made it so popular that other restaurants wanted it.

➤ When I began franchising, my thought was to give restaurant owners an item of food they could serve their customers with pride.

➤ By the restaurant owner taking care of his customers' interests, the owner's interest is taken care of—and my interests are inevitably taken care of.

➤ I do hope that you will have only the customers in mind at all times."

John Y. Brown first broached the possibility of his becoming involved in Kentucky Fried Chicken when he accompanied the Colonel to Frankfort, Kentucky, to examine a barbecue restaurant the colonel was considering as a possible franchise opportunity. "We went over to Scottie's BBQ together," Brown said, "but I said, 'Colonel, I'm a salesman. I've been selling all through college. And I'm a lawyer. Let me set this up and we'll be partners.'"

But the Colonel demurred. "The fellow who has never had experience cuttin' up chicken or fryin' chicken just wouldn't know how to talk to a fellow who's runnin' his own restaurant and workin' in the kitchen sometimes himself. He might have no business havin' the chicken franchise."

Instead, the Colonel offered him a chance to buy into the new barbecue franchise. "So I signed an agreement with him," Brown said, "and we were going to be 50-50 partners in the restaurant. I was going to raise the money and run it. He also gave me the right to put in Kentucky Fried Chicken."

Soon after reaching an agreement with Colonel Sanders, Brown struck up a conversation about his business aspirations with Jim Kavanaugh from Nashville, whose wife had been Eleanor Brown's roommate in college. Kavanaugh quickly saw the possibilities with both the Colonel and the franchise operation.

"He was a young fellow, and he was probably impressionable," Brown said later. "He got someone to come see about financing my first store. I didn't have any money, nor did I know how I was going to get it. So Jim brought Jack Massey in. He was retired and had a little finance company with his father. I picked Jack up at the airport and went into my law office. We negotiated for three hours over a half a percent because he had to pay the Kavanaugh people something for introducing me. Finally, after three hours, he said, 'Well, it doesn't look like we can do a deal.' I said, 'Now Mr. Massey, you sit down there, we're going to do a deal before you leave here.'"

The two men hit it off, and Massey financed a $16,000 equipment package for Brown's restaurant. "And that's how I got started," Brown said. He opened the Porky Pig House in Louisville with Ona May Barbati, who had once worked with the Colonel in Corbin, along with her husband, Joe. John's wife Eleanor made the curtains while he cooked and waited tables.

Just before the restaurant opened, the Colonel visited the new establishment. He carefully examined the barbecue pit, which was so new that the mortar was still wet. Brown said the Colonel sniffed disdainfully, said "It isn't worth a damn," and knocked it all down with his cane.

And while the restaurant was named the Porky Pig House, it also featured Kentucky Fried Chicken, and it quickly became obvious which meat the public preferred. At the end of the first reporting period, Brown's books showed that the restaurant's volume was 80 percent chicken and 20 percent barbecue. John Y. Brown immediately met with Jack Massey and told him, "Jack, you know, somebody is going to buy the Colonel out. He's seventy-four years old." They decided the time was right to make a move.

Negotiations Begin

"The first time I took Jack up to meet the Colonel, we went out to lunch. The Colonel said, 'No city slicker is going to come in here and buy my business.' I just wilted. He'd had a bunch of rogues in there trying to buy him out, but no one really legitimate. Some guy who was going to buy it went off and stole a boat or something—there are all kinds of stories."

"'I'm not interested in selling," the Colonel told them. "And if I ever did decide to dispose of the business, I would make it available to the franchisees on some basis or another." Massey cited examples of how that concept had failed with other franchise operations, but the Colonel didn't budge. When pressed for details on his plan to sell the business to the franchisees, the Colonel said, "I would get Pete Harman, Kenny King, Phil Clauss, and some of the other larger franchisees together, and I'd ask them what they'd like to do about it," the Colonel said.

Brown and Massey spent three months trying to convince the Colonel to sell, visiting family members, friends, and franchisees. Their hook was that they would guarantee that the larger franchisees could purchase large blocks of stock and serve as members of the board of directors of a new corporation.

Massey and the Colonel never fully liked or trusted each other, but both of them trusted Brown. Finally, in October 1963, they came to an agreement in principle. Massey guaranteed $160,000 in bank loans for Brown and put up the rest of the $500,000 for the down payment himself toward a buyout price of $2 million. But the Colonel wasn't ready to sign.

"The more I thought about the idea, the more I could see it had some good angles," the Colonel said later. "Brown and

Massey didn't know the difference between a drumstick and a pig's ear. But Pete Harman did, and since he was a franchisee himself, he would also be lookin' out for the welfare of the franchisees.

"Brown was young, and if he gave his life to developing the franchisee business for Kentucky Fried Chicken, he would have many years to contribute. He also had the vision for a world-wide organization—and, I thought, probably the enthusiasm for developing it. Massey was a financier. He had money himself, and probably he knew how to raise more. So finally I reached the conclusion that I'd go along with them on the sale."

"We offered him $2 million," Brown said, "then we went down to Jack's bank. But the bank president said, 'Why don't you offer him a million and a half?' I said, 'If you offer the Colonel one dollar less than $2 million, he's going to walk out of here and raise Cain.'

"I didn't have any money, but I did sell them on the idea that if it's worth $1.5 million, it's worth $2 million. So we went back in and said, 'Colonel, we're going to offer you the $2 million you want for your business. He sort of stroked his chin, and said, 'Okay.'"

The Colonel then held up a hand—and John Y. Brown said his blood froze. "He said, 'I'm not going to sell until we talk to Pete Harman.'" Harman, the first franchisee, was still the man the Colonel trusted most in the world.

Pete Harman—Trusted Friend

"We had to sell Pete on the theory that someone had to take the company and manage it," Brown said later. "Otherwise, the franchisees would end up taking over the company and fighting each other. He agreed with that."

The Colonel, Massey, and Brown all arrived in Salt Lake City on January 5, 1964. It was Jack Massey, not John Y. Brown, who stayed up all night drawing up the initial contract on three pages of a legal-sized yellow pad. The contract called for a half million dollars down, then a million and a half over six years at 3 percent interest.

"The next morning, Pete met with us, and I think he probably wasn't crazy about it because we weren't from the chicken school or the family," Brown said. "But he also recognized that this would be good for the Colonel and probably good for the company. There was a little sense of, 'Gee, I wish *I* could do this. (But) you all seem like nice people, so I won't stand in the way of it.'"

> *"The Colonel had really brought some dogs out here before Jack Massey and John Y. Brown. Jack Massey was probably the most impressive to me at the time, but John Y. had the vision."*
> —Pete Harman

The four men met at the Harman Café on State Street at 6:00 AM. Brown said that all four reached agreement and that checks were written for the sale price.

"Jack asked me, 'How much do you want to make this for?'" Brown recalled. "We were paying $50,000 down. I said, 'Just make mine $10,000'—not knowing where I was going to get the $10,000. But Jack and I had an agreement that we were partners, and he was going to finance my part of it. I was going to attempt to run it, and he was going to sort of be a mentor. But he would be out of the day-to-day business."

Grateful for his support, Brown and Massey offered Harman 5 percent of their new corporation's stock. Pete also retained exclusive rights in the state of Utah. The new company would be called Kentucky Fried Chicken, Inc. It had the right to develop the business throughout the world, save for Montana, which already had been sold; Florida, which had been given to Sanders' daughter Margaret; Utah, which the Colonel awarded to Pete Harman; Canada, which the Colonel kept; and England, which was owned by Ray Allen.

Brown and Massey then contacted another early, influential franchisee, Kenny King. The original plan was to offer Kenny a 5 percent share for $25,000. But while King was doing well with Kentucky Fried Chicken, his restaurants were still full-service operations. King and his attorney declined, and

Brown and Massey returned to Louisville to wait for the Colonel to sign.

Feeling the Pressure

"We sat there for two months," Brown said. "This is my chance of a lifetime. Jack had some lawyer down in Nashville, they were piddling around with the contract. I didn't understand about stock and the purchase disclosures and all that. I just thought if you had a deal, you drew it up. I was not a corporate lawyer, so I didn't know why it was taking two months. And I was scared to death because every day the Colonel was sitting in the back saying, 'I'm going to call it off if y'all are going to screw my company out of all of these things.'"

The pressure was having its impact on the Colonel as well. "During the next two months before the final deal, I went through hell," he recalled. "I suppose I was a pretty ornery cuss around the house and in the office. I was afraid something would happen to the product and to the people who had helped make it popular when I turned it over to folks outside the food business. And I let Brown and Massey know how I felt about it, too. But when March 6 finally came, I gritted my teeth and signed the final papers."

After he received the money, the Colonel dictated a professional, erudite letter to Brown and Massey that was contrary to the "country" manner of speaking he had adopted in public.

> "It is my intention to deliver to you the best and most conscientious service I can render, consistent with my health, as long as I remain on your payroll. I can see no cause for anything ever arising again to cause the heartbreaks we have endured for the past eighteen months. The business is yours to operate as you please, and I will never be critical to anyone other than you two about how you operate it. Anything that I suggest to you would be merely a suggestion, and no hard feelings on my part if they are not taken. I wish you both health and happiness from this day on."
>
> —Harland Sanders

John Y. Brown Jr. had not been idle during those days spent waiting for the Colonel to make the sale official. He made several far-reaching decisions during those crucial early months. First, he went to the publisher of the *Louisville Courier-Journal.*

"I said, 'I don't know whether you know it or not, but the Colonel has sold his business to Jack Massey and myself.' The next day they came out, had a photographer that took the Colonel's picture and mine, then it was all over the United States. Then it was a lot easier to move on and get it closed without him backing out or not wanting to do it. But if Pete had not approved our initial sale, I don't think the Colonel would have done it at all."

The New KFC

Brown also quickly moved to shape the new company in his own image. He started by hiring a young, New York City-based public relations expert, Stan Lewis. Lewis's strategy from the start was to promote the colorful Colonel, whom he booked on the most popular television shows of the time.

And once the contract situation was settled, Brown began to build his own team of "lean, hungry, bright young men"— most of whom he'd played poker with, but few of whom had any experience in food service or restaurant franchising.

Brown and Massey also began assembling a board of directors, all of whom were named honorary "Colonels" in KFC's promotional materials. Pete Harman was named the first vice president. Other directors included Maurine McGuire, Ervin Hanks, Philip Clauss, and the Colonel's grandson, Harland Adams. Massey was named board chairman, while Brown's title was executive vice president.

Another one of Brown's early innovations was the formation of a national advertising co-op where each franchisee was required to contribute $250 that first year. The company would match that amount, and the first year's budget was

$235,000. To induce franchisees to contribute to the fund, Brown gave them control.

An Unhappy Colonel

"When I finally signed the papers in Pete Harman's restaurant, it was clear as hell to me that Canada was to be my area of operation," the Colonel said. "But it wasn't long before I heard the company talkin' about goin' into Canada. They said the lawyers interpreted the wording of the contract to mean that I was the only one who could *process* chicken in Canada, but that the company had the right to *merchandise* it. "I didn't care how the lawyers interpreted it, that wasn't what I meant when I signed the agreement.

"Anyway, when they paid me the first installment of $500,000 on the $2 million sale price, they gave me the remaining stock of the company to hold as collateral for their note on the rest of the money to be paid. Then, with the rapid growth of the company, they decided to go public with the corporation. Their only problem was they needed the stock that I had in my safety deposit box in the bank."

"'Colonel Sanders,' they said, 'we need to have that stock so we can enlarge the business.'

"'You won't get the stock until you give me a clear-cut contract to operate Kentucky Fried Chicken in Canada,' I told them.

"So the lawyers got together—theirs and mine—and clarified the wordin' in the contract so that I had the right to process *and* merchandise, and do anything else with Kentucky Fried Chicken in Canada.

"So when that was clear, I went to my safety deposit box and gave them the stock."

Shortly thereafter, the Colonel founded a nonprofit charitable foundation, Harland Sanders Charitable Foundation of Canada, then deeded all of his stock in Colonel Sanders Kentucky Fried Chicken of Canada, Ltd. to the foundation. All profits over administration expenses were to be donated to charity.

In the years that followed, the Colonel continued to agonize over the sale, openly wondering whether he had done the right thing in letting his "baby" go into the hands of strangers. Some believed that the Colonel was not properly compensated for his creation. Still others claim that Massey and Brown smooth-talked the Colonel out of accepting ten thousand shares of stock, allegedly claiming that it would be better to accept cash for tax purposes.

But John R. Neal, an early franchisee and former KFC employee, claims that the decision was the Colonel's alone. "The Colonel was very uncomfortable with the idea of some kind of shares in the company," Neal recalls. "He never believed in this stuff called 'stock.' Consequently, he never made the millions and millions everyone else made."

Years later, the Colonel ultimately told *Advertising Age* that he didn't regret the sale—or the sale price.

> *"Last year (1977), KFC did $1.5 billion worth of business. What the hell would I do with $1.5 billion? It'd just make a pile of money for me and the government. When you get to the cemetery, you can't do business from there."*
> —Harland Sanders

"I sold my business because I didn't have anybody to succeed me to run my company. At my age in life, I thought that would be enough to take care of me and Claudia both. I've remained with the company and make $200,000 a year. That's the same as the old (U.S.) president's salary, isn't it?

"All I need is enough to enjoy life. I'm just plumb satisfied, just as happy as I can be. I don't have a care in the world. Me and Mr. (Jimmy) Carter are in good shape."

Whether devils or saints, the Colonel eventually settled with Brown and Massey for $2 million, plus an annual retainer of $45,000 (later $75,000, eventually $200,000) to serve as a good-will ambassador, along with residuals from all television commercials, which he later donated to one of his favorite colleges.

Although he was serving as a figurehead and quality-control expert for this "new" Kentucky Fried Chicken, the

Colonel remained one of its greatest assets. He continued to travel the country, meeting people, promoting the secret recipe, and promoting the company. His instincts for success also remained uncanny.

According to *World Franchising* magazine, among those he met in 1963 was Englishman Ray Allen, a former sales manager in the textile industry. Ray became the first English franchisee, and by 1973 he had an interest in more than fifty company-owned stores and oversaw 150 franchise units. Allen was one of the new company's great success stories.

Building the New Company

John Y. Brown Jr. was equally industrious during those critical early years of the new Kentucky Fried Chicken. John Y., who was deathly afraid of flying, logged more than a million air miles, visiting every franchisee in the country, trying to get them all to sign a standardized contract.

Brown and Massey asked that franchisees pay 3 percent of the store's gross. They also demanded a more standardized approach to the franchise operations. And, like the Colonel and Pete Harman before him, Brown realized that someone who has equity in a company is going to work harder. He gave stock—then valued at fifteen dollars per share in 1964—to key employees and arranged loans so others could buy it.

When a franchise began to falter in Dallas, Brown persuaded the board of directors to purchase it in 1964 and continue operations as a company-owned store. Within three years, Kentucky Fried Chicken owned a hundred stores, although individuals still controlled 1,512.

"All I did was travel around the country and get people on the same contract," Brown recalled. "The Colonel had an agreement that paid him five cents a chicken, which with inflation would have been two cents a head, in ten–fifteen years. I spent seven months on the road having seminars and franchise meetings. Every franchisee but one switched over to the new contract. I just couldn't get him switched over.

"On about my fourth trip down there, I got him to sign. Then he woke me up at four in the morning, telling me his wife didn't like the deal. I said, 'Jim, I'm asleep in here, and I've got to call *my* wife before I make any changes on this.'

"It was a fair deal. It took a lot of selling, but everybody was making money."

Brown's other far-reaching decision was based on the success of the freestanding, take-home-only stores pioneered by Pete Harman in Utah and Margaret Sanders in Florida. He required all future franchisees to adopt a standardized model. The new stores would emphasize fast service and would lower labor costs dramatically as a result.

Franchisees in the Carolinas built what were Kentucky Fried Chicken's first "standard" image restaurants in late 1963. The buildings looked like Southern plantations, complete with white columns in front and long roofs with two spires or cupolas at the top, à la Churchill Downs. Some franchisees placed weathervanes shaped like the Colonel, complete with his cane, at the top of the spires/cupolas. Brown insisted all new franchises adopt a uniform look. In the years to come, new designs would be implemented.

John Y. Brown's tumultuous relationship with the Colonel continued on a sometimes rocky road in subsequent years. Harland Sanders—fiercely independent, a perfectionist, a short-tempered genius, an artist—would often find himself at odds with the men and women trying to turn his dream into an empire. It was a collision between vastly different cultures that often barely understood each other. They were two sometimes feuding forces united only by a single aim—to serve the best damn fried chicken in the whole world.

> "He liked people, and he liked promotional work. He was a natural showman. Anytime he could get out front, promote something, get all the attention, that was him. But once he got it going, someone else had to keep it going. He wasn't a natural manager."
> —Claudia Sanders
> (the Colonel's wife)

The Colonel on Television

The Tonight Show with Johnny Carson
The Mike Douglas Show
What's My Line?
I've Got a Secret
The Merv Griffin Show
The Dave Garroway Show
The Lawrence Welk Show
The Jerry Lewis movie, *The Loudmouth*

The Colonel was a star overnight. Everybody in the country with a television set started seeing Colonel Sanders all over the place. Still, Brown had his reservations. He looked on the Colonel as something of a loose cannon. "Every time the Colonel would get on one of those shows, I'd get so nervous I'd almost pass out. But it never bothered him at all. He loved it. He was such a great natural actor. We'd be backstage, waiting for him to go on, and I'd keep reminding him to say this and say that, and he'd say, 'John, quit worrying. I know what to do.' And when his time came, he just pranced out there like he'd been facing the footlights all his life."

"When you get down to it, that was the secret. He'd been preparing for this all his life, waiting for his chance, knowing what he could do if he had the chance, waiting to act on a stage big enough to fit him."
—John Y. Brown

Every time the Colonel appeared on national television, there was a distinct jump in sales. Ultimately, the Colonel appeared on thirty-one national TV shows, including a spot dancing on Lawrence Welk's show. "That's what really launched us back in the early days," Brown said. Harman agreed. "The Colonel had done well for us on a local level. Once John got him on national television, that was a real turning point."

Like Harman before him, Brown realized that the success or failure of Kentucky Fried Chicken was as much tied to the public's accepting and embracing of the Colonel himself as it was to the taste of the chicken itself. He later called this "The Big Idea"—and it eventually paid enormous dividends for all concerned.

Harman Moves into California

Later in 1963, when one of the Colonel's original franchisees let his contract for Northern California lapse, Harman snapped it up. "We had this huge opportunity for four big counties where most of the population is in Northern California. So we asked Chuck and Twila Kern to open the first store on Arden Way in Sacramento.

Just like the two most recent Harman stores, the Kerns built a stand-alone Kentucky Fried Chicken restaurant. A giant billboard towered over the building with a full-length Colonel and the words "Colonel Sanders Recipe Kentucky Fried Chicken" and "It's finger-lickin' good" prominently displayed. Much smaller, and just above the entrance, the words "Harman Take Home" were paired with a picture of the Colonel's mug on one of the ubiquitous buckets.

"They had to buy chickens about forty miles away," Harman said. "They would have to go pick up their own chickens and haul them down every day, but Kentucky Fried Chicken really took off in Northern California."

One of Harman's first calls when he moved into Northern California was to his advertising wizard, Alan Frank. Frank had just returned from a week's vacation when Harman called him, saying, "I've been looking for you. Where were you?"

"Well, I took a week off, Pete."

"While you were gone, we bought Sacramento."

"Why do you want to go over there? You're doing so well with your stores in Utah."

"Because I want to create more opportunities for more people," Pete said. "We've got that market now, and I'm taking you along."

Aggressive advertising was going to be Harman's chief strategy in Northern California, and Frank was going to help him carry it out. For Sacramento, Harman and Frank decided to promote the opening with a half-price sale—a one-dollar box of Kentucky Fried Chicken for fifty cents. "We blew the roof off," Frank said. "People were lined up down the street for a block and a half. We were so busy *I* had to run the cash register!

> *"Loyalty just doesn't exist in this country as much as it should. Pete is all about loyalty. So when Harman's expanded to handle Northern California, I was there."*
> —Alan Frank

"Pete understands that you deal in volume. He said, 'I'd rather sell a thousand buckets of chicken at $3.50 than seven hundred at $4.50. He understands food and paper costs—he always knew what he was doing. He had a great sense for business, even with his lack of formal education."

With the success of Arden Way, Harman began expanding at a rapid clip. He built or acquired a new Kentucky Fried Chicken restaurant at the astonishing rate of one every twenty-eight days until he had one hundred restaurants.

A host of trusted employees in Utah were among the first to own their own restaurants in California, taking the "Harman family" concept along with them to each grand opening.

The Harman photo albums are full of pictures from the California stores. One photograph shows long lines of people outside the Stockton restaurant in 1963—all waiting for three pieces of chicken, French fries, and rolls for fifty cents. An advertisement from the newspaper touts the Sacramento store's first anniversary and three stores—2212 Arden Way, 6514 Franklin Boulevard, and 3672 J Street. Still another photo shows Keith and Miriam Holmes happily munching Kentucky Fried Chicken at their restaurant in San Bruno where, during their opening half-price special—they sold 4,100 boxes of chicken.

While the purchase of Kentucky Fried Chicken by John Y. Brown initially had little impact on Harman, in 1966 he took the important step of forming a management corporation to oversee his thirty-one restaurant outlets in Utah and California.

Harman, of course, was the first president of the new Harman Management Corp., with Parley Jacobsen as the first comptroller. Alice Hardy was named vice president/general manager over all Utah operations, while Lex Overzet held the same position in California. By this time, California was home to twice as many restaurants as Pete had in Utah.

Harman's decision to incorporate was a direct result of this rapid expansion into California. He had to have capital to propel the growth. In addition to providing a large line of credit, the new corporation allowed Harman to follow his first loves—providing opportunities for more people and experimenting with new food concepts.

The following year, the Colonel was a surprise guest at the Harman organization's Founder's Anniversary. Seven of the original forty employees from Harman Café were in attendance and received engraved silver plates: Betty Allen, Jerry Conover, Nila Washam, Alice Berry, Julia Bennett, Virginia Gee, and—of course—Alice Hardy.

Not pictured was one of Harman's newest employees, a strapping young sixteen-year-old, Jim Olson, who began as a fry cook at Harman-Sunnyvale that year. Olson's career is a paradigm for Harman Management, a textbook example of how employee empowerment and management insight can produce exemplary results.

"I took a friend in to get a job at KFC, and I filled out an application at the same time—almost by accident," Olson recalled. "I was playing sports and didn't plan on working. When my coach and I had a disagreement, I decided to quit playing basketball. And KFC was the thing to do if I wasn't going to play sports. Like most things in life, people find their courses almost circumstantial."

Jim's story is typical of many Harman employees. It started as an after-school summer job. But something kept him—a sense that somebody cared about him, beginning with his store managers.

And where Olson's story diverges from the great mass of such stories in American life is that at Harman Management, young people like Jim Olson were viewed as future leaders. As was usually the case, Olson met Pete Harman himself shortly after joining the Harman family.

"He walked in the back door," Jim said. "He had on that old Colonel string tie, and I was scraping a filter for the shortening. Pete walked up and asked me what I was doing. I thought 'Well, that's pretty dumb. I'm scraping the filter. What do you think I'm doing?' But I noticed everybody else in the restaurant acted a little differently, so I thought he was maybe the truck driver or something because he didn't have any great airs about him. He was just kind of an average guy walking through the store.

"When he left, I asked 'Who was that guy?' They said, 'That was Pete Harman.' I said 'Who's that?' I didn't even know who the owner of the restaurant was. I thought, 'Boy he didn't act like an owner.'"

Although Olson planned to eventually attend college, he liked the responsibility of running a restaurant at age seventeen. "In other jobs, you were told to do your job, shut up and let the adults do their thing. With Harman's, the young people were challenged to do more and take on responsibility.

> *"When we hire kids to come in and work for us, more than likely it's their first job. It's the most important job they'll have in their lives. And if they take their job responsibilities seriously, it builds confidence within them so that they can move on to other jobs."*
>
> —Pete Harman

"I liked that feeling of somebody counting on me. I liked the feeling of being responsible for other people. And even though my parents wanted me to go to school, and I was going to be the first college graduate in my family, there was something intriguing about running that little business unit and seeing what you could do all on your own."

Olson continued working at the restaurant for fifty-two dollars a week while attending San Jose State University, gaining valuable people skills every step of the way.

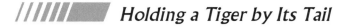

Olson interviewed with Hewlett-Packard and other cutting-edge companies upon graduation in 1972, then made an appointment to meet with Pete Harman. "His attitude was totally different than the other interviewers," Olson recalled. "His question was, 'What can you do to make people better?' That was the first question he asked me. 'What can you do to make people better?' I don't even remember what I said.

> *"When he said those words—'What can you do to make people better?'—I thought, That's me! This is what I want to do."*
> —Jim Olson

"In one class I had taken at school, they take you through how to respond in an interview. And that wasn't one of the questions they prepared me for. That threw me. Instead of thinking about your ego in the company, it was thinking about other people. That was consistent with how Pete had always treated me in the past."

In the years to come, gangly young Jim Olson would systematically work his way up the Harman Management ladder—all the way up.

6

Wall Street's Darling

The years that followed subjected KFC to a dizzying array of emotions—millionaires were made, companies were moved, risky new ventures were launched, and John Y. Brown's frequently controversial tenure came to an end.

But through it all, the heart and soul of KFC—Pete Harman and the Colonel—continued to preach a simple, unadorned gospel:

Serve up food that's so good it brings customers back.

Perhaps it wasn't as sexy as strolling the floors of the New York Stock Exchange or bankrolling daring franchise concepts, but, in the end, that concept continued to bring loyal customers through the door.

In the end, Brown discovered what the long-time franchisees and employees back at the corporate headquarters knew all along—it's all about a unique product, one's that's served fresh with consummate care and pride.

Everything else is just window dressing.

When the man in the white suit strolled onto the floor of the New York Stock Exchange, action halted for the first time in history while traders roared their approval of Colonel Harland Sanders. He bought the first hundred shares of Kentucky Fried Chicken and started a stampede.

It was 1966, and the company finally was going public—much to the satisfaction of Wall Street, which had been waiting to pounce. Pandemonium ensued. Stock that had been selling for ten to fifteen dollars a share quickly jumped to a hundred dollars a share and, with stock splits, eventually sold for $400 a share. The skyrocketing stock price generated a buying frenzy unmatched until the tech stocks of the late 1990s.

By John Y. Brown's estimate, the stock splits created 150 instant millionaires. Jack Massey's initial investment became worth more than $35 million. The Colonel's long-time secretary, Maurine McGuire, who had invested five thousand dollars, suddenly found herself worth $3 million. Brown said that Pete Harman's stock was suddenly worth $15 million, while he himself was reportedly worth substantially more. The following day, of Kentucky Fried Chicken's three hundred Louisville employees, Brown said twenty-one were millionaires—and all reported directly to him.

"I didn't know anything about organizational charts and all that. They're all talking about their boats and depreciation and how they didn't want to go to Seattle—that's too far. They became a bunch of prima donnas," Brown said. "Finally, I called them all and said, 'Look: y'all don't understand what it means to be a millionaire. Most people never get the chance.' Maybe 1 percent of the population at that time was millionaires. I said, The president of the United States, Richard Nixon has a net worth of $243,000. I understand he's been president for however many years, he was vice president for eight years, and he's only worth $243,000. So while y'all have a big swagger about how smart you are, let's understand two things:

"The reason that we're all millionaires is the Colonel looked good and the chicken tastes good."

But chaos reigned at corporate headquarters. At one point, Brown recalled that his wife Eleanor pulled him aside and whispered, "You ought to fire them all."

"I should have," Brown said. "I should have gotten rid of the whole lot of millionaires and started over. In any event, they were a lot of good people. They just didn't fit the corporate environment because they had made their own money (and) they'd run their own businesses.

"My biggest problem was I didn't know where to find the people to help me run it."

For John Y. Brown, operating a business had proved to be more difficult than actually acquiring it. "We just grew so fast that we couldn't really develop management," he said. "I was young and naïve, and there wasn't anybody to steal an employee from. There wasn't a Wendy's or a Taco Bell. There was only McDonald's and ourselves. We brought in the franchisees. Even Dave Thomas worked for us for close to two years. But they didn't fit in the corporate environment. They were all talking about doing their own thing.

"The Peter Principle finally caught up with me. After three years, we all decided that I needed to learn how to run a business. I'd just gone to law school and sold encyclopedias, and I didn't learn anything. We were just figuring things out; I'd hired a bunch of guys I'd gone to school with, what I thought were hard workers, smart, and honest."

In desperation, Brown went to Harvard Business School and lunched with eleven professors. He told the story of Kentucky Fried Chicken, since most of the professors at the time had never heard of the Colonel. He said he talked about take-home restaurants and chicken in a bucket and a secret original recipe. When he was finished, one of the business professors said, "Mr. Brown, how are your sales?"

He replied, "Well, we've gone from about $3 million to a little over $100 million."

A second professor frowned and asked, "What about your profits?"

"He was wondering why would I be there unless we were having some problems," Brown said. "So I said, 'We've gone from about three hundred thousand dollars to a little over $10 million, pre-tax.'

"The host looked at me, and smiled, and said, 'Mr. Brown, you just go back and keep doing whatever you're doing, and don't let us confuse you.'

"That's the first time I realized we knew more about our business than anybody else—except the Colonel."

KFC Moves to Tennessee

Brown may have known "our business," but he didn't know human nature. One of his missteps was—at the urging of Jack Massey—moving Kentucky Fried Chicken, Inc.'s corporate headquarters to Nashville.

The first headquarters of KFC had long been located on rolling Kentucky hills outside Shelbyville, in the heart of thoroughbred and tobacco country. The site was split among the Colonel's rambling ten-room home, the more modern general offices, and a large warehouse. New franchisees invariably became part of the "KFC family," staying and dining with the Colonel and Claudia.

The relocation pleased Massey, who had family and extensive holdings in Nashville. He believed that Nashville's higher profile would enable it to attract stockholders. Although Brown was against the move (his family lived in Louisville and it was a draining commute), it was Massey, after all, who had put up most of the money.

When the decision to relocate was announced, the Colonel spat fire. He shouted, "This ain't no damned *Tennessee* Fried Chicken! No matter what any slick, silk-suited SOB says!"

The Colonel continued to operate out of Shelbyville, visiting Nashville only when absolutely necessary. Margaret Sanders wrote that Brown had promised her father that Kentucky Fried Chicken would never leave the state. "Father raged, 'Those sons-of-bitches are crazier than hell, trying to sell a Kentucky product out of Tennessee!' In addition, it left Father with a huge empty office building in his backyard."

Pete Harman also questioned the decision and worked tirelessly behind the scenes to get Massey to reconsider.

According to Alan Frank, Massey also insisted that a Nashville-based agency, Noble-Drury, be awarded the advertising contract as the agency of record on a limited contract with a ninety-day cancellation clause.

"It wasn't long before I started calling them 'Noble Dreary,' because they were not too good," Frank said. "I was president of KFC's advertising co-op, and I convinced the committee that we should hire advertising agency people like myself as consultants. I appointed agency reps from Los Angeles, Chicago, Detroit, and Baltimore to serve on the committee as consultants.

"Finally, in 1969, I convinced both Jack Massey and John Y. Brown that, if they were going to go big time, they really ought to start looking at national agencies." Later that year, the committee hired the Leo Burnett Co. in Chicago as the advertising agency. "That's when things started to roll," Frank recalled.

Among Burnett's many memorable commercials for KFC was a little beauty from 1972 that boasted the instantly hummable "Get a bucket of chicken, have a barrel of fun" jingle written and performed by none other than Barry Manilow.

Other chains tried to jump on the fried chicken franchising bandwagon. Competitors included:

> Minnie Pearl Fried Chicken
> Maryland Fried Chicken
> Daniel Boone Fried Chicken
> Chicken in the Rough

But all eventually wilted and faded before KFC's relentless advance. "Looking back, we had a lot of entrepreneurs, and I guess if we had at that time stopped and had a slower growth, maybe we'd have done better," Brown said. "But at that time we were the only game in town. My philosophy was, 'Let's just blitz the market.'"

Among those who joined in the blitz were National Football League stars Alan Ameche and Gino Marchetti, who in the 1960s owned forty-nine stores in Baltimore and Philadelphia alone.

> *"Even as I've gained wisdom over the years, it's hard to find good people. It's better if you can grow them out of the business like Pete Harman—but if you get them off of résumés, you're just shooting in the wind."*
> —John Y. Brown

Despite inexperience at the corporate offices, Kentucky Fried Chicken continued to grow. In 1967, *Business Week* wrote that Brown and Massey had transformed the "loosely knit, one-man show . . . into a smoothly run corporation with all the trappings of modern management." Or so it appeared, anyway. Retail outlets reached all fifty states and a dozen foreign countries.

Still frustrated on the management side, Brown threw himself into what he knew best—aggressive expansion. This suited his mostly entrepreneurial staff. The country also embraced the franchise concept. In 1968 alone, Brown said, Kentucky Fried Chicken built 861 stores, an industry-wide record that co-opted KFC's new breed of competitors. "We ran fastest and got there first," John said later. "They were too late."

Today, Brown is quick to give credit to the Colonel for KFC's early successes.

> *"I got all the credit for these developments, but actually the Colonel had had the idea for almost every one of them, long before me. That's one thing that people forget about him; a lot never knew it. He was an extremely inventive, innovative, imaginative man. He was always thinking up marketing ideas, publicity gimmicks, sales ideas. You get a man that creative, he's going to be sensitive, emotional."*

KFC University

Brown also sought guidance from Pete Harman and Jackie Trujillo. Just as the Colonel once taught Trujillo the proper way to fry Kentucky Fried Chicken, Brown came to Salt Lake City to learn from Jackie. Using the training manual codified by Trujillo, he then established the first "KFC University."

Admission to the university was guaranteed as part of the new $3,000 franchise fee. Typical start-up costs for a new Kentucky Fried Chicken restaurant—now sporting the uniform, prefabricated, red-and-white striping—were around $65,000 in 1967.

He also began a policy whereby one of the company's twenty field representatives checked on each franchisee once every three months to smooth out any problems and ensure quality control. The KFC engineering department was given additional control over all technical aspects of the cooking equipment and its maintenance.

Eventually, most of the new millionaires left, and Brown frantically began to hire business school graduates.

"We ran into trouble later when I started hiring all those corporate professional managers that came in with a book under their arm like they really knew everything," he said sadly. "They didn't know anything. Most of them were out of work or about to lose a job, and we filled the hallways with them. None of them were worth shooting. So it was really almost like starting from scratch and building an organization.

"During that time, I grew very fond of the Colonel. I never had an argument with the Colonel. He argued with everybody because that was his style of management. But any time he'd get riled up with me, I'd just change the subject and he'd forget what he was mad about. I loved him. He was a brilliant man with a great idea. I listened more to him than all those professional managers that we brought in."

But, as Brown grew increasingly insecure about the management side of the business, he turned more and more to those new professional corporate managers for advice.

Still, according to Jackie Trujillo, Brown did have a successful model he could have followed—Pete Harman's. "John simply didn't have the pool of loyal, well-trained employees that Pete did," she said. "Jim Olson, Vern Wardle (who began as a dishwasher in 1967 at 39th South and State), and myself all would walk through fire for Pete. Nor did John have the same kind

> *"We only do two things well: We celebrate and we motivate."*
> —Jim Olson

of relationship with his suppliers. Once you worked for Pete Harman, you always worked for Pete Harman."

Back in Nashville, a new cadre of MBA-trained managers worked diligently to present a more polished image to Wall Street. And, along the way, some bright young marketing genius decided that the Colonel himself was an anachronism. Unbeknownst to Brown, he recommended that the Colonel be phased out, and he suggested that the way to do it was to cut the Colonel's pension. Although the suggestion was never acted on, the Colonel somehow heard about it.

Brown's Biggest Challenge

"I didn't know what a pension plan was and I'd never worked for a company," Brown said. "The night before one of our conventions, I stayed up all night playing gin rummy with one of our franchisees, George Baker. I hadn't been to sleep. That was not unusual for me in my early days. I wrote my speech out on a seven-page yellow pad the next afternoon.

"The Colonel had been stewing about this pension plan that he was supposed to be cut out of, and we had a contract with him for forty thousand dollars year. I should have known something was up—he wore a black suit. Before a crowd of a thousand people, he got up and spent forty minutes berating the ownership. He said that we didn't know what we were doing, that we were out for their money, that we don't know anything about the chicken business, and that we were changing the recipe. He went on a tirade. He said, 'This young Brown boy, he's still wet behind the years. And Jack Massey is . . .' I don't want to use the term, but he used very salty language."

> *"The Colonel is an artist. And like all artists, he's a perfectionist. He founded this company on the desire not just for profit, but for excellence—and on the belief that if you give your customer the best you can, you will prosper."*
> —John Y. Brown

Brown was the master of ceremonies and, like most of the crowd, sat stunned during the Colonel's rant. This was an important convention for the new ownership. Most of the 1,000 people in attendance knew the Colonel—but not John Y. Brown Jr. When he finally took the microphone, Brown said, he knew he faced the most critical speech of his career.

"You know, the Colonel is very demanding, and he's going to have to expect the best of us. Let me say this, Colonel: we've tried to honor you, your goals and dreams. I just want you to know that every deal that you made with these franchisees here, we have honored. We've honored every one of them 100 percent.

"Also, Colonel, we haven't raised the price, because we respect your relationship with these franchisees and tried to give them a good deal. And we haven't had a lawsuit. McDonald's got thirty of them over there. We've put every effort into getting along positively with the franchisees. We love you, Colonel, and we're going to reach out and continue to try to live up to your expectations."

Brown outlined Kentucky Fried Chicken's explosive—and lucrative—growth, and how the franchisees had made more money from KFC stock than the company had taken from them in royalties.

"Colonel," Brown said, "you're still our leader. You'll always be our leader. And I give you my word that we're going to make this company all you want it to be and more."

Brown's off-the-cuff remarks in a dangerous situation drew a standing ovation.

"That was sort of my moment of glory, I guess," Brown said. "The next morning at breakfast the Colonel—now back in his white suit—said, 'You did a good job last night, Johnny.'

"The Colonel is a talent. That was his style—whether he had $2 million or $200, it didn't make any difference to the Colonel. He was an artist, and I wanted to treat him like that."

But the convention marked a turning point in the franchisees' perception about just *who* ran Kentucky Fried Chicken.

The public responded and sales continued to soar—fueled, in part, by a catchy new advertising slogan: "We fix Sunday dinner seven days a week."

To maintain the momentum, Brown raised the advertising contribution to fifty dollars per store in 1968—then increased it to 1 percent of a store's gross per month.

In addition to trying to manage and promote a company that was now Wall Street's darling and a host of new millionaires, Brown was hopelessly infected with the "entrepreneur's disease"—he wanted to do it all over again. Or, as he said in an interview at the time, "Sooner or later, we were going to run out of places to build chicken stores."

Considering Fish

Encouraged by the response of American tourists at his father's fish-and-chips shop in northern England, Haddon Salt and his wife Grace came to the United States in 1965 hoping to franchise their concept. Soon there were more than a hundred H. Salt, Esq. Authentic Fish and Chips restaurants—mostly in Southern California.

Brown bought the concept from Salt for $12 million in 1968. The Salt operation was appealing for a number of reasons, but what most attracted Pete Harman was the aristocratic presence of Haddon Salt, whom he believed could be marketed as an English version of the Colonel. After meeting Salt at his store in Sausalito, Harman contracted for the Bay Area franchise. Eventually, he would operate forty-one restaurants in California, Colorado, and Washington.

"When we started, we used to pay fifty cents a pound for fish," Harman said. "We bought our fish out of Scandinavia, and so we went over several times on trips and made good contacts. I liked it so much I later tried a few Kentucky Fried Chicken outlets in Denmark.

"Eventually, I think we were paying about sixty cents a pound, which was still fairly cheap. But boy, sales were good. Particularly on Good Friday, we would have people lined up down the street. We did really well in San Francisco, where we had quite a few stores. We opened the back door up for a line and sold out the back door *and* the front counter."

In 1970, Brown boldly planned to have a thousand H. Salt, Esq. stores by 1973. But, unlike chicken or even cattle, the price of fish is directly tied to a number of factors, most notably oil prices. As the price of oil rose in the 1970s, it directly affected the H. Salt, Esq. chain.

"Then the price of fish went to two dollars a pound instead of fifty cents," Harman recalled, "and then you had to raise your price to match that to pay for the expensive fish. And the public just wouldn't pay it."

Secondly, unlike Kentucky Fried Chicken, the H. Salt concept was going up against an established seafood chain, Long John Silver's, which featured both a more varied menu and in-house dining. And finally, fish simply doesn't travel as well as fried chicken. Fish quickly becomes cold and soggy long before it reaches a picnic site or the beach.

Harman slowly began divesting himself of the stores. Incidentally, the H. Salt, Esq. Authentic Fish and Chips chain survived and still remains strong, particularly in Southern California.

Considering Beef

Brown's second idea was to sell beef. The Colonel had already considered the idea when Brown came along. His foray into beef began as early as 1964, when he searched for someone to head up his still-unnamed new division. Eventually, Brown settled on long-time KFC franchisee Kent Prestwich to head up Kentucky Roast Beef Company, a division of Kentucky Fried Chicken Corporation, in 1968.

Brown agreed to continue the brand, in part because he believed that most of the prime areas for KFC franchises had already been filled. He also believed that roast beef allowed the company to grow even faster through diversification in the field it knew best—fast-food service. The concept was blessed with an oversized, eye-catching sign, featuring the Colonel's already legendary mug (but with a rakish chef's hat) over the words "Kentucky Roast Beef" and, in smaller type, "Kentucky Ham."

According to KFC promotional materials, the pilot store in Las Vegas was successful enough for Brown to open more stores. During the first twelve days of operation, the initial operation averaged about $2,500 per day, while volume at a nearby Kentucky Fried Chicken store remained unchanged.

The franchisee fee for the new concept was $10,000, with a franchise royalty on gross sales set at 3 percent. The pilot building in Las Vegas cost $50,000 and franchisees were required to attend a five-day training course at the new Kentucky Roast Beef Training School in Nashville.

The concept flourished briefly, reaching one hundred stores, but eventually dwindled away until later owners quietly closed the remaining restaurants. By October 1971, *The National Observer* had already dubbed both the fish and beef concepts as "unprofitable."

For a time, Brown even dabbled in motels. On September 5, 1969, he announced ambitious plans for a chain of Colonel Sanders Inns.

> *"During this period, Kentucky Fried Chicken got away from its core strength. Cooking the best chicken should be enough. We should have stayed with it exclusively. We did chicken better than anybody in the world."*
>
> —Pete Harman

As if to prove Harman's contention, following a trip to Japan, Brown's first tentative stabs at establishing Kentucky Fried Chicken overseas generated positive results. Soon the company was represented in seventy-nine foreign countries.

Back to Louisville

When Jack Massey announced his retirement at age sixty-five, after selling most of his stock for an enormous profit, Brown announced that he was moving KFC back to Louisville—much to the Colonel's delight.

Building soon began on new corporate offices at 1441 Gardiner Drive, on the outskirts of Louisville. Designed to look like a Kentucky colonel's plantation, the handsome white building with the stately columns actually resembled one of Washington, D.C.'s better-known landmarks. It was quickly dubbed "The Whitehouse." Kentucky Fried Chicken's new International Headquarters Building opened September 16, 1970. Within two years, the Louisville office had exploded to 343 employees.

In April 1971, the first Colonel Sanders Inn opened, virtually in the Whitehouse's front yard. It would eventually become a Holiday Inn, as this concept also withered on the vine. "The real reason we stopped building the inns and got rid of the ones we had was that the investment was too big for the return—and, about the time we were ready to expand, the money dried up," Brown said later.

Apart from Kentucky Fried Chicken, Brown became one of five owners of the new American Basketball Association franchise in Louisville, the Kentucky Colonels. After some initial success, the Colonels also began to struggle at the box office, despite Brown's best efforts.

Brown faced more serious issues in 1970. Several observations first noted by stock market analysts in the late 1960s eventually became public record in 1970. First, accountants reported that, for most of the industry, profits for successful franchisers came from company-owned stores—not from independent shops. While this was not true of Kentucky Fried Chicken, Inc., it soured some investors on the chain.

Second, a report in *The Journal of Accountancy* regarding how initial franchise fees were applied caused another reaction on Wall Street. And franchisers, once the "glamour stocks" of the 1960s, found rough sledding in 1970. Even Kentucky Fried Chicken, Inc., which had hit a high of $55.50 in 1969, fell to as low as $10 a share the following year.

Third, the country entered a period of recession that would impact every sector of the economy.

Brown used his considerable personal charm to woo Wall Street and the press. He confidently raised the royalty for new stores to 4 percent of gross. And, in an interview with the *Wall Street Journal* in April 1970, Brown dismissed the sharp drop in the price of KFC stock. "Wall Street is having convulsions without any prognosis," he said. "The way they're selling the stock, you'd think the public has given up eating chicken and all the housewives have gone back to the kitchen."

He characterized Kentucky Fried Chicken, Inc. as "a solid company that intends to become the blue chip of the fast-food industry. (We've) taken unfair abuse because of the promotional nature of numerous companies in the industry. We've been in business fifteen years and we have never had a failure. We've always met our 'Street' estimates and our accounting is conservative. We're not going to worry about results on a quarter-to-quarter basis, but concentrate on building a lasting, strong concern. And I expect to weather the temporary slump and come back strong because our earnings will be there in the future."

Still, the turnover continued at the new headquarters in Louisville. Four vice presidents resigned in April 1969, although it was rumored that Brown threatened to fire them all if they didn't. In August, even the Colonel, his grandson Harland Adams, and George Baker all resigned from the board of directors.

The Colonel, nearly eighty years old, told *The New York Times* that he knew he was in over his head on the board. "I realized that I was someplace I had no place being. Everything that a board of a big corporation does is over my head, and I'm confused by the talk and high finance discussed at these meetings."

Unfettered Growth

Brown, meanwhile, was everywhere, talking to the press, shoring up stockholders, frantically hiring new people. Among the new employees were R. C. Beeson, chief operations officer, who replaced George Baker; and Joseph Kesselman, chief financial officer. Kesselman brought in new marketing, controlling, and computer experts and obtained the company's first large-scale loan package. He also effected a style change—convincing Brown to stop wearing a string tie to work.

"I had a lot of good instincts for acquisitions," Brown recalled, "but I didn't have anybody that could evaluate the companies, much less run them. I had really more than I could handle, and I didn't have a number-two guy, nor did I have the organization that could either take over the acquisitions or manage the company.

"I've never enjoyed being an entrepreneur because you're always building and you're never quite there. The more successful we got, the more hoops we had to jump through. First, we're dealing in all fifty states, and then we're going public, and then we're dealing international. Looking back, the pressure was always on me."

By the end of 1970, Kentucky Fried Chicken operated 3,400 fast-food outlets, including 823 company-owned stores. The company, once too big for the Colonel, grew too large for John Y. Brown Jr. as well.

John Y. Brown Sells to Heublein

Hoping to smooth hurt feelings over the abrupt departures of the Colonel and his grandson from the board of directors, Brown chose the Colonel's eightieth birthday to announce the grand opening of KFC's Whitehouse. Brown invited the Colonel and all Kentucky Fried Chicken franchisees. Brown said he wanted to invite representatives from Wall Street as well, but some of his senior staff objected.

"One of them said, 'Johnny, you shouldn't invite Wall Street down here,' Brown recalled. 'They'll see this new building, all these oriental rugs, the molding, all this fancy expense you've got here.' I said, 'Really, you think?' He said, 'Yeah, they'll just say you're wasting money.'"

"I almost thought I'd call them off, I didn't want to cause any problems, and our stock had dropped enough. Well, I didn't. They came down and our stock went from ten to nineteen dollars in three days. Then Heublein walked in and and offered us twenty-four to twenty-six dollars a share.

"That's when we sold out because I had really run out of people. I didn't know where to find them. There wasn't any other company I could go hire them from. So, I guess I sort of sold out of exhaustion."

The sale would not be final until July 1971. A *Wall Street Journal* article on the sale had mixed marks for Brown's tenure. "In engineering Kentucky Fried's explosive growth," the article stated, "Mr. Brown neglected to install needed financial controls and food-research facilities, and had let relations with some franchise holders go sour."

Brown's legacy with Kentucky Fried Chicken is mixed. He instinctively relied heavily on franchising, which enabled the company to avoid the high costs of expansion and still keep his shareholders happy.

And since he, like the Colonel and Harman before him, believed that his managers should have the same opportunity to get rich in the business that he had enjoyed, the wildfire growth meant plenty of promotion and stock options for managers. It also enabled franchisees to spread their administrative costs over a larger operational base—and improve *their* profit margins as well. This meant Kentucky Fried Chicken remained an attractive option for possible franchisees and investors, regardless of the current stock price.

Conversely, by the time the company was fielding serious purchase offers, the corporate staff was already both dispirited and riddled with unfilled openings. Even the field force had been reduced to a skeletal operation. The Colonel was unhappy. And the franchisees, while mostly successful, were disenchanted as well.

In retrospect, Brown said it was the relations with the company's diverse, independently minded franchisees that was his favorite memory of the job. Thirty-five years later, many of them still have fond memories of the man who would eventually parlay his experience at Kentucky Fried Chicken, Inc. into the governorship of the state of Kentucky.

"I really was fond of all the franchisees, and I always felt like I was giving them a square deal," Brown said. "I'm very close to them.

"I didn't have any other choice when it came time to sell. When Heublein came in, all my corporate people loved it. They got their benefits, they worked five days a week. Back in the old days, we worked seven days a week—we'd be there until eleven or twelve at night.

"I didn't know about politics in corporate life. I never realized everybody wants to get next to the throne, and everybody is backstabbing everybody else. I went through that learning experience, and I learned better by the time I became governor. But I wanted to please everybody. It was a very frustrating time of my life."

In the end, Brown lavished credit for whatever success he enjoyed primarily on two men:

> *"If you really want to give credit for this, you give the credit to the old Colonel, because he really had the idea. But Pete Harman was the one who paved the way for all of us. He was the one who proved the concept. He was the best operator of the bunch. He came from the same school as the Colonel did—he liked getting back in the kitchen and being sure all that food was right."*
>
> —John Y. Brown

The Colonel in front of a 1970s restaurant

The Heublein Takeover

In the years that followed, KFC changed hands again, this time to a giant international company. Not for the first time, attention to the small things that had made KFC a truly outstanding brand wandered. And when that happened, the business suffered. For the Colonel, Pete Harman, the hundreds of franchisees and thousands of long-time employees, the answer was surprisingly simple. It was a lesson that would need to be repeated occasionally throughout KFC's history:

Success is in the details—every penny counts.

But during what would become the first "re-colonelization" of KFC, another secret would emerge. And like the hard-won business insights that preceded it, it was one that would have a significant impact on the company as a whole in the future. The answer to a corporation's problems sometimes aren't global in nature. Sometimes those answers can be found in the exacting execution of the smallest of day-to-day operations:

If you lose quality, you lose it all.

On July 8, 1971, Heublein purchased the Kentucky Fried Chicken Corporation for $285 million. On that date, more than 3,500 franchised and company-owned KFC restaurants were in operation worldwide. The billion-dollar Heublein Company had been an odd choice to purchase Kentucky Fried Chicken. Begun in 1875 by brothers Gilbert and Louis Heublein in Hartford, Connecticut, Heublein was best known as the importer of the world's best-selling vodka, Smirnoff.

Despite Heublein's lack of experience in quick-service restaurants, Pete Harman and others were initially optimistic about the purchase. They hoped that a first-class, well-run operation like Heublein could bring order out of the chaos of the final years of the John Y. Brown regime. Harman also was intrigued with Heublein's international expertise—its products were marketed in more than one hundred countries.

> ### Notable Heublein Products
>
> *A-1 Sauce*
> *Harvey's Bristol Cream*
> *Lancers Vin Rose*
> *Black Velvet Canadian Whiskey*
> *Jose Cuervo Tequila*
> *Grey Poupon Mustard*

"Plus, we were hoping that Harman Management might expand abroad as well," Pete said. "It appeared to be a good mix at first." According to franchisee LaRue Kohl, the initial impression of the sale among the many smaller franchisees was equally positive. "We were very snowed by them, because they really courted us and took very good care of us in the beginning.

"The franchisees were a pretty diverse group," Kohl said. I don't think in our area that we were looking for much national help. Still, we were pleased that they at least recognized us and paid a little attention to us. We didn't see many hands-on things. Our new corporate inspectors would come in from Heublein, and they'd know less about what was going on than we did. In time, we didn't see any real help out of Heublein— but I don't think we really anticipated any."

"I liked Heublein's commercials and print advertisements, particularly those for Smirnoff," Harman said. "They were considered among the best in the business—smart, funny, slick, and very contemporary—although there was a feeling among some of the franchisees that KFC's image was a little old-fashioned."

After the KFC takeover, Heublein immediately restructured into three separate operating groups:

1. The alcoholic beverage import division
2. The international division, which included all Heublein operations outside of the United States, as well as all company-owned KFC stores overseas
3. The consumer products division, which included Kentucky Fried Chicken and A-1

Harman liked Barry Rowles, the man Heublein initially placed in charge of KFC, who promptly appointed Pete to the Heublein board of directors. Rowles told Harman about his plans to broaden Kentucky Fried Chicken's menus, upgrade the now-dated company stores, and aggressively expand overseas.

"But he didn't say much about the Colonel," Harman said. "That should have been a warning signal. Plus, Heublein was still struggling financially to get United Vintners back on its feet. So I don't think we got all of the attention we needed in those early years. Plus, we had our first real competition— Church's Fried Chicken. Church's was doing pretty well with its crispy chicken—but the Colonel would have none of that."

Rowles, like most of the new leadership, obviously had little sense of the company's history—or the Colonel's impact, according to Harman.

The Colonel on World Peace

Upon hearing that Soviet Premier Nikita Khruschev had been forced out of power and was ailing, the Colonel acted. "Well, he is now out of work. They wore him out and then they put him out. Now he's sick. His problem is he ain't working. I'm going to go over there and teach him how to cook my chicken—get him back on his feet." The Colonel was actually en route to Moscow when word arrived that Khruschev had died.

"The Heublein people didn't really understand or appreciate the Colonel," Brown said. "They were corporate people. They didn't respect what he had done. Didn't know. They were going to cut him out of their ads. They told me that they hadn't made up their minds whether they were going to use the Colonel or not."

Pete's Words of Wisdom

▶ There is no substitute for treating your people fairly. I always wanted every person who ever did business with me to want to do business with me again.

▶ I like to perpetuate our system of ownership. There are just not enough work-oriented people involved in ownership in our free enterprise system.

▶ The emphasis on hard work and the free enterprise system to achieve success is a shared philosophy between the Association and myself.

▶ I believe in the future of this country and the opportunities that continue to be available to all who are willing to dedicate themselves to their goals.

Even though there were thunderclouds on the horizon, life at Harman Management was bright and sweet as a day in May. It was on May 12, 1971 that Pete Harman was invited to join the Horatio Alger Association. Harman took the stage with nine other new members, including commentator Lowell Thomas and Robert Henry Abplanalp of Precision Valve Corp. Most of Harman's brothers and sisters joined Pete, Arline, Barry (and his wife Elaine), and Dawnie at the Waldorf Astoria Hotel in New York to witness the event. According to Alan Frank, the Colonel was there to lead the applause.

For the man who had spent most of his life giving recognition to others, this was a supreme moment. Just as he'd always shared his success with others, Harman spent most of his time sharing this moment in the sun with his family and coworkers.

Back at their new home near Los Altos, California, Pete and Arline took a day off to tend to their horses, then resumed work, planning his first expansion overseas.

Harman Heads Overseas

Through his fish-and-chips outlets, Harman had been encouraged by what he'd seen in Europe. With Heublein's blessing, he opened three stores in Denmark under the direction of Einar Bertgstedt. Harman also sent Bill and Pat Peden to coordinate quality control and training, Alan and Beverly Frank to coordinate promotions, and Bruce and Sally Garner went as managers.

"We went to Denmark while we were up there buying fish for the H. Salt stores," Pete said. "It's quite a long country. You have to go in a boat to get around. But I liked the people, and thought they'd go for the chicken.

"Our first store was in downtown Arhus, and it really took off. Our people phoned back home and said, 'We've got lines around the corner! We've got to have some help! These people don't know how to work at the speed we're used to!' So we got the fastest passport that was ever issued out of San Francisco—three hours—and we put Jim Olson on a plane for Denmark. He was there the next day."

For the past year, Olson had been store manager of the KFC across the street from Harman Management's new headquarters in Los Altos. The restaurant had been founded as a training school for all Kentucky Fried Chicken outlets in California, and Olson trained any new managers who hadn't grown up in the Harman system. At the end of two weeks under Olson, the new managers were thoroughly indoctrinated into what Pete called "The Spirit of Harman."

"I took them through a course that would train them in all the basics—from preparation to company policies to food safety to various procedures," Olson said. "The goal was to make sure everybody has the same training before they get out into the restaurant program."

Olson's success meant that he was the first person Pete Harman thought of when the cry for help came from Denmark. Upon arriving, Olson moved quickly to get the operation in working order, and business boomed as a result. Pete then opened a second store, this one in Copenhagen and managed by Jim and Sherry Thornton. It was followed by yet another store in Alborg.

For all of his marketing and promotional skills, Alan Frank found Denmark a difficult market, since there was no commercial television at the time. "The government owned television, so the only way you could advertise was with magazines and billboards," Frank said. "There wasn't even commercial radio."

Frank developed a series of funny commercials featuring a talking puppy that would continually interrupt the announcer.

"It really got their attention," he said. "We were telling a story. It was very successful. Every newspaper and magazine wrote about it. But that was short-lived because to keep top-of-mind awareness about your product, you've got to be promoting it day-in and day-out."

Eventually, despite an appearance by the Colonel, sales dropped off at all three restaurants. "Fried chicken just didn't catch on over there," Harman recalled sadly. "Denmark was known for little sandwiches, very good delicate sandwiches, but the chickens just never took off." Eventually, all three stores were closed.

Imperious Dictates

KFC had established its first store in the Far East in 1970 in Osaka, Japan, as part of Expo-70, and by 1973 it had sixty-four restaurants in Japan, mostly in Tokyo. Fifteen more stores followed in Hong Kong, with additional openings following in Australia and South Africa.

But new Heublein directives to establish more uniformity—and more stringent controls—on both U.S. and foreign stores soon precipitated a clash with local managers. Japanese KFC restaurants successfully offered fried fish and smoked chicken, while their South African counterparts successfully offered hamburgers. Also, the rapid expansion had meant that not all restaurants had experienced managers. By 1975, management problems forced Heublein to close all of its restaurants in Hong Kong.

It wasn't much better in the United States. Heublein's imperious dictates did not sit well with the decidedly independent franchisees. Soon, most of the remaining top managers hired by Brown and Massey were either fired or quit. Sales dropped company-wide. And, not surprisingly, the sale of Kentucky Fried Chicken to Heublein had been hard on the Colonel primarily because Heublein sold alcohol—and the Colonel *hated* "demon rum."

To make matters worse, Heublein felt strongly that the chain needed to add crispy chicken to counter the threat from Church's. When Brown initially asked the Colonel to promote a new extra crispy chicken, he refused to allow his name to be attached to the product. But Heublein went ahead with the plan anyway.

The Colonel Attacks

"It's my face that's shown on that box of chicken and in the advertising. It's me that people recognize, and they stop me everywhere I go to complain. The damn SOBs don't know anything but peddling booze, and they sure as hell don't know a damn thing about good food!"

—The Colonel

The Colonel had taken potshots at Brown and Massey as early as February 14, 1970, in a widely reprinted article from *The New Yorker*. But it was with the purchase by Heublein that he began to fire both barrels on a regular basis. Then, angered by what he considered the decline in quality of food service everywhere, the Colonel decided to open his own restaurant in Shelbyville with his wife, Claudia, called The Colonel's Lady's Dinner House. When he announced that he was going to franchise the concept—and sell Original Recipe chicken—Heublein protested. The Colonel immediately filed a $122.4 million suit, alleging that Heublein had interfered with his franchising concept.

The suit was ultimately settled out of court. John Y. Brown had a hand in the settlement, convincing Heublein that the Colonel deserved more money. In return, the Colonel signed an agreement to cease and desist attacking Heublein in public. It worked—for a while. But in 1974, the Colonel urged two nephews to start their own chicken business, Famous Recipe Fried Chicken.

> "If he decided he wanted to charm you, you might as well roll over, you'd done been charmed. He could do that. If he decided that he didn't want to have anything to do with you, he didn't have anything to do with you, simple as that."
>
> —John Cox

The Colonel resumed publicly sniping at both Heublein and individual franchisees. Most of his comments received only regional media coverage until September 1976, when the Colonel paid an unexpected visit to a company-owned store in Greenwich Village—accompanied by a *New York Times* writer. The Colonel raged against the quality of the food, calling the mashed potatoes "wallpaper paste," and claimed, "That's the worst fried chicken I've ever seen." The story made national front pages.

Anthony Tortorici, then director of public affairs for Kentucky Fried Chicken, responded gamely. "We're very grateful to have the Colonel around to keep us on our toes. But he is a purist, and his standards were all right when he was operating just a few stores. But we have over 5,500 now, and that means more than 10,000 fry cooks of all ages and abilities.

"The Colonel has very high standards of personal conduct and for his product. We need wider parameters to adapt to the real world. But I guarantee if you go back into that store, you'll see big improvement."

It was a public relations nightmare. Rowles couldn't respond without putting KFC in the untenable position of attacking its namesake founder. The franchisees, many of them old friends of the Colonel, pleaded with him to stop his attacks, which hurt them and their bottom line.

In the end, it took the combined efforts of three people to settle the wider dispute, Shirley Topmiller, John Cox, and Pete Harman. The man in the middle was John Cox, who originally had worked for Heublein, left, and rejoined the company in 1972, when he was assigned to Louisville as director of public relations (and later, VP of Public Affairs). He knew it was going to be a challenging assignment:

"I followed a guy who had been the Colonel's buddy. I thought, 'John, wear your asbestos underwear, because this isn't going to be good.' I became the umbilical cord running between the Colonel and the corporation and vice versa.

In the end, we had a good relationship, I liked him and he liked me—which didn't mean we often agreed, particularly after *The New York Times* article. People were angry with my bosses at Heublein, the franchisees were angry because he maligned them and the system, and my bosses here were unhappy."

Cox pulled out the settlement with the Colonel and underlined each place where the Colonel was in violation. He took the agreement to a birthday party at the 21 Club in New York that the Colonel was going to attend. Cox quietly ordered everybody out of the room.

"I said, 'Colonel, you're going to go to that birthday party and sugar will not melt in your mouth. Now let me tell you something. If you're really lucky, Heublein isn't going to come and get its million-dollar settlement back from you, and it isn't going to fire you. It isn't going to put your restaurant in Shelbyville out of business. Let's just go to the birthday party and have a wonderful time.'

"So he did. Everything was fine, everything was smooth, everything was 'Hello there, honey' and 'Hi, sweetie, how are you?'

"Then he came back to Louisville for a birthday party with the franchisees, which was kind of a strained event, as you might expect. Some of the folks at Heublein wanted to fire him, but Barry Rowles and I persuaded them that it's pretty hard to fire your trademark. We asked, 'Do you really want him running around the country with no controls whatsoever? If you thought he was pissed off before, wait until now.'"

Finally, the Colonel and Claudia met privately with Cox. "He brought Claudia in because he thought I wouldn't beat him up verbally with her there," Cox recalled. "I didn't beat him up too bad, and I was glad to have her there because she had more control and, in many a sense, was a better business-person than he was. We went on from there.

> "Workin' is better than rustin,' so I'll keep workin.' I've got fourteen more years to finish this century, and then I might retire. I want to have a few more years as a senior citizen."
>
> —The Colonel

"My job was to keep the Colonel under control, and I failed miserably at that for years and years. Shirley Topmiller did a much better job. She'd say things like, 'Oh, now, Colonel honey, you don't want to do that, do you?' —meaning 'You *aren't* going to do that'—and making it stick." Cox believed that much of the Colonel's unfocused anger during this period stemmed from a feeling of inadequacy when dealing with a multinational corporation like Heublein.

"He had basically no education, and he felt that acutely," Cox said. "He was most comfortable with people who had no education. He was most comfortable with children. We would go anywhere and they'd appear. I remember going into a TV studio in the middle of the day. We sat down to wait, and in five minutes there were five children who came out of the woodwork. I don't know where they were, I don't know what signals echoed through the building, but there they were.

When Heublein bought the company from John Y. Brown, Cox said that the Colonel believed he'd only traded enemies. It was that perception that Cox worked daily to change. "Of course there always was the tension that ran between the franchisor and the franchisee everywhere. The franchisee thinks the company is out to screw them, and the company thinks the franchisee isn't trying hard enough. They have different objectives. The franchisor wants to get revenues up because that's where his royalties come from. The franchisee is interested in cash flow. That's how he lives and buys things.

> *"He had a big, soft heart. He liked old people, too. Everybody else he figured should be able to take care of themselves. He would do almost anything for kids."*
> —John Cox

"Although I think it was better after I came, anytime there was any kind of conflict between a franchisee and the company, the Colonel would take the franchisee's side. I think after I arrived, he came to trust me. Eventually, he would look more at the merits of an issue rather than a reflexive, 'I'm on his side' kind of thing." But it was a slow, painstaking process.

Despite Cox's best efforts, it was obvious that the Colonel's rants were detrimental to all involved, from the franchisee with a single store to Heublein itself. At one point, both John Y. Brown *and* his father got involved—Brown Senior visiting the Colonel and Brown Junior visiting Rowles, urging both parties to make peace.

Shirley Topmiller

A second influential figure who helped forge a truce between the Colonel and Heublein was Shirley Topmiller. She was first a secretary, then a public relations specialist at KFC. She went on to achieve legendary status around the Louisville offices.

Topmiller, recently divorced with two small children, suddenly found herself in need of a job in 1971. Since she lived near Kentucky Fried Chicken's Louisville headquarters, it was the first tentative stop on her quest.

"I thought this would be a good place to go to work if I could, because when my children got home from school they won't be there too long without me," she said. "And if I had to run home, it wouldn't be too far. I had all of these insecurities. I pulled up to KFC headquarters early one afternoon, sat outside in my car in front of the building, and said a prayer, 'Lord, you know what I'm going through here. Just help me. If this is the place you want me to be, you're going to have to open this door and make this work.'"

As she walked to the front door, someone pressed past her and opened it for her.

The Colonel said, "Well, little lady, someone as pretty as you, I should know."

Topmiller smiled and introduced herself. She, of course, recognized the Colonel.

When he asked her what brought her to KFC, Shirley told him she was job hunting.

The Colonel nodded and replied, "Well, good luck to you" and went on his way. But the receptionist in personnel indicated that there were no openings. Topmiller shrugged and left to run a few errands. By the time she'd returned home, the personnel office had called, asking her to start immediately.

A few months later, Topmiller asked how she'd suddenly been offered a job when it originally appeared that none were available. The personnel officer replied, "Oh, the Colonel came back here and wanted to know where we had put you. You should have seen it—not one person wanted to say we sent you home. So we were just scrambling to get you."

Thirty years later, Topmiller said she still feels blessed. "I have to tell you, all those years that I worked here, I felt like I was exactly where I was supposed to be, because what I had prayed for worked out. I came to work every day knowing I was exactly where I was supposed to be."

Topmiller quickly moved up through the organization until she was assigned to work with Cox, who by then directed both the franchising and public relations departments. And working in public relations meant working with the Colonel.

Shirley Topmiller was exactly the right person to work with the Colonel.

"Mr. Cox came to me one day and said, 'You know, you seem to be the only person in this place that he likes. Don't give up the work you're doing now, but would you just do his travel schedule? Let's see how it works.'

"The first time the Colonel was in town, John introduced us formally and said, 'Shirley is going to do this.' He left us alone for a few minutes, and I said, 'Colonel, you know I'm a single mother here with two little girls. I cannot lose my job. So you and I have to figure out a way to make this work. I want you to promise me that you're not going to go out and talk bad about the company—it all comes back on us. I just want us to work together, and I need your support in that.' He promised me that he would.

"After that, he and I just got along beautifully. He had to pass my desk every time he went into John's office, and even when he was in a bad mood—and that was frequently—he was sweet and kind to me. We never, ever had a cross word. I think I'm the only person in the whole world that can say that. I just loved him, and I know he loved me, and we had good times together."

But it wasn't long before the Colonel was railing against Heublein and Kentucky Fried Chicken again. Whenever that happened, Cox sent Topmiller to intercede. "I could figure out that he might veer off the path that he promised me he'd stay on, so I'd say something like, 'It's you and me, Colonel, against the world. It's you and me against these corporate big guys.' That worked. He loved that. He had a real partner, he felt. John also was a partner, but John had to represent more of the corporate side than I did.

"I would just say things like, 'Colonel, you're smarter than these reporters. Don't let them get you talking about the gravy. Don't do that—they just want a big story. Don't give it to them.' I could tell that he started to see things a little differently rather than always being so feisty and wanting to always have a little controversy about everything. It went very well."

But still the Colonel persisted in his attacks on Heublein. Finally, alarmed by what he was continually hearing and reading, Pete Harman quietly began working on his old friend. "I loved the Colonel," Harman said. "He loved me. He called me 'Honey.' He'd come through town or I'd stop in Shelbyville and we'd talk. I cashed many a Social Security check for him in the old days. I told him that he was hurting the franchisees. He was hurting Heublein—I know, because I was on the board. And he was hurting himself. He was worrying himself into an early grave. I told him it was time to let it go. Eventually, it took all of us working together, but I think we got to him."

> *"America loves what the Colonel cooks."*
> —KFC trademark, 1974
>
> *"Have a barrel of fun."*
> —KFC trademark, 1975
>
> *"Visit the Colonel."*
> —KFC trademark, 1977

According to Cox, that's exactly what happened. The Colonel couldn't bear the thought that speaking his mind was hurting Pete Harman and his beloved Kentucky Fried Chicken. In the end, it was a meeting of minds between two old business partners and friends who had endured much together and formed an unbreakable bond that forged a truce.

"In the old days, the Colonel would have a prospect in his room talking to him," Cox said, "and suddenly Pete would come barging in. He'd shout, 'Colonel, I can't believe the sales we're having!' And he would be waving his 'sales results'. 'Another record week!' Suddenly, Pete would see he'd interrupted a conversation, apologize and back out. And whomever the Colonel was selling would get big eyes and say, 'Oh, wow! You can make that kind of money in this business?' Later, the Colonel would get another prospect in and here Pete would come running in again—'Colonel! I can't believe how well I'm doing!' It was a flimflam, but it was an honest flimflam. It was show business.

"Pete said the Colonel took him on several trips around the country. He would pick up Pete, and Pete would always go.

Pete never made any money out of it—he did it just because he loved the Colonel.

"Pete was as important to the establishment of the company as the Colonel was. Did he get something out of it? Sure he did—he got a highly successful business in Utah. Did he contribute something? You bet—he's the one who really made it happen. It's one thing to have a product, it's another thing to have the launching pad.

"Pete was the ultimate master of people skills."

And he needed them all to calm the Colonel. Ultimately, Cox, Topmiller, and Harman convinced the Colonel to tone down his complaints.

If You Lose Quality, You Can Lose It All

In retrospect, the Colonel's concerns were not unfounded. Behind closed doors, Harman expressed many of the same sentiments to the rest of Heublein's board of directors. Food quality was suffering, too many stores were dated and less than spotless, and the Colonel was being squeezed out of the equation completely.

Consequently, Heublein's relationship with its KFC franchisees was frosty at best. Franchisees sold considerably more per unit than company-owned stores *without* Heublein's help. They resented paying royalty fees to an ineffective corporate parent. And, as other chains began to edge into the marketplace, sales dropped. While Heublein focused on overall store sales, they didn't notice that the basic chicken business was slacking off. The successful introduction of barbecued spareribs in 1975 only delayed the inevitable.

To ensure that his stores avoided the malaise infecting so many of the other KFCs, Pete instituted the "Mystery Shopper" program in 1976. He found qualified individuals outside of the chicken business and sent them to Harman restaurants armed with an extensive checklist. "They go around and check the restrooms," Harman said, "then they'll order two or three items, and they'll eat them inside the restaurant.

"You can't use the same ones very often because once in a while our people would notice that someone *acts* like a mystery shopper, and it can get around the whole system pretty fast. But a mystery shopper is a good deal because you get somebody from outside Harman's organization to go in and check the service. They check everything from the drive-through windows to how long it took for them to be greeted when they entered the store. Probably the most important thing they check are the restrooms and the uniforms. And the store manager gets all the reports—even before we do."

John B. Mann, a former director of product development for Carnation, had been named KFC's vice-president for research and development in 1975. He liked the Harman Mystery Shopper concept and instituted KFC's version later in 1976. Mann told *Institutions* magazine that KFC's situation was desperate. "We used to go into a store and try to guess who would speak first. We were surprised if a store was good. Things were so bad that one Christmas dinner, we all prayed."

Like Harman Management's Mystery Shopper, Mann insisted that his inspectors be completely separate from operations, with "no axe to grind."

Although the program evolved over the years, by 1980 six full-time inspectors covered all 765 company stores at least once a month, along with one hundred franchised stores. In four years, the average score—a total based on everything from cleanliness to friendliness to product temperature readings—rose from the low 70s to 93 out of 100 possible points. Still, Pete admitted that the Mystery Shoppers confided to him that they always enjoyed visiting Harman Management stores the most.

"They're always telling us how surprised they are at the family feeling that they run into at Harman's. They tell us that everybody works together, and of course the reason why they do is that everybody starts at the bottom of the company. I don't think there was any period of time that we went into a big slump, even in the mid-1970s. You might hit a recession, but we always do well when things are tough."

The Colonel once worked on the railroad.

Harland and Claudia Sanders at the service station
he opened in 1930 in Corbin, Kentucky

Top:
Interior of the
Colonel's original
restaurant in
Corbin in the late
1930s

Left:
Pete Harman's
Aunt Carrie

1944 — Pete and Arline at Earl Carrol's Vanities in Los Angeles

Left:
Pete, Arline,
and son, Barry
(two months
old), in San
Francisco

The Do Drop Inn, circa 1941

Pete bought brand new uniforms for his South State Street carhops in 1954. L-R: Sharon Thoreson, Jolene Bronson Wignall, Miriam Gutke (Holmes), Janet Park, Connie Barrus, Jackie Bills (Trujillo), Grace Cooley, Virginia Gee.

One of the billboards advertising the first bucket

World's first KFC located at 3890 South State Street in Salt Lake City

1962 — Employees of Harman's 39th South Restaurant
L-R back: Betty Kihlstrom, Lois Jonas, Jackie Trujillo, Virginia Gee, Vi Shore, Dee Gerbich, Marlis Moe
Middle: Barry Harman, Betty Allen, Betty Holtman, Sunny Reynolds, Mary Cawley, Lou Creger, Anita Moore, Alice Hardy, Pete Harman
Front: Rosa Lee, Beulah Garner, Jean Nelson, Shirley Hamblin, Lorraine Webster, Twila Kern, Edith Akers.

Pete and Arline with the Colonel, 1962

Norman Vincent Peale, the Colonel, Jack Massey, John Y. Brown

1963 — Jack Massey presents Pete with the Distinguished Service Award.

1967 — Grand opening of Harman-Palo Alto (later renamed
Harman-Paul & Donna for the restaurant's original managers)

Pete and the Colonel in Louisville

Top:
KFC Restaurant
Support Center in
Louisville ("The
Whitehouse")

Left:
Pete and the Colonel
outside of Harman
Cafe in 1968

The Colonel was at home in the kitchen, where he
repeatedly experimented with recipes.

Dedication of the Caroline Hemenway Harman Building at BYU in 1982

November 12, 1987 — KFC opened this 3-story, 12,000-square-foot restaurant in Tian'anmen Square in Beijing, China, directly across from Chairman Mao Tsetung's Mausoleum.

Top:
Children celebrating the grand opening of the 500th KFC restaurant in China

Left:
Pete stands beside a pyramid of 5,000 buckets, commemorating the opening of the 5,000th KFC restaurant in 1990 in Daly City, California.

Top:
Two girls enjoy Kentucky Fried Chicken in front of the Zhengyangmen Gate-Tower in Tian'anmen Square in Beijing.

Left:
1990 — Pete is the Gold Plate Award recipient from the International Food Service Manufacturing Association (FMA). He was selected as Food Service Operator of the Year.

L-R, Don Parkinson, former Vice President of Franchising, Pete Harman, and David Novak, then KFC President. Pete receives the Promise Pride Award

Left:
Pete and Arline celebrated their 50 years in the restaurant business on August 22, 1991 in San Francisco.

Top Left: David Novak, Tricon Chairman & CEO
Top Right: Cheryl Bachelder, KFC President

Harman's executive team (L-R) Vern Wardle, Vice President of Operations;
Jackie Trujillo, Chairman of the Board & CEO; Pete Harman, Founder; Jamie
Jackson, Vice President of Finance; Jim Olson, President & COO (photo taken
at Harman's 2000 Top Ten)

Even though the buildings have changed over the years, the Colonel's mug has remained the icon. Above is a 1960s restaurant; below is today's KFC.

Beginning in 1974, Heublein also found itself embroiled in negotiations over a new contract with franchisees. Taking point for the franchisees was John R. Neal. Neal had been president of KFC International from 1967–1970 when he left to become a franchisee himself. He was elected to the National Franchisee Advisory Council in 1974, then became chairman of the NFAC's Contract Committee.

"When Heublein bought the business, they didn't know anything about meeting customers," Neal said. "They were packaged-goods people. KFC was a franchise, dependent on entrepreneurial American men and women facing the consumer every day. The management team up in Farmington didn't really understand that. They really didn't understand the redneck franchisees that you find down here in the southeast. What they did was just milk the business, run the stores down, and damn near ruined the KFC brand."

Two years later, in May of 1976, the two sides were at an impasse while meeting on Amelia Island, off the coast of Florida. "The demands we wanted were very clear," Neal said. "We wanted a cap on the royalty at 4 percent. We didn't want them to tax us every time we turned around. We wanted a cap on the advertising at 5 percent. After the twenty-year contract expired, we wanted automatic ten-year renewal rights for as long as the franchisee would bring its store up to standard. So, if he did a good job, he'd be able to extend that contract without having to start all over again.

> *"Success is a wonderful thing if you don't hog it. There are enough kinds of success in this world so everyone can have some."*
> —Pete Harman

"The other critical point of the contract was a mile-and-a-half exclusivity, where we'd be able to have nobody come any closer to us than a mile and a half. We had gotten the mile and a half, but we didn't have the cap on the royalty, the cap on the advertising, or the ten-year."

Heublein was represented by KFC President Jim Wille, John Cox, and others. Suddenly, Neal said he was called into a hotel suite where Wille and Cox sat at a small table.

"They said, 'John R., if we give in to these demands that you and your team have made, will you call off your membership and support of the Moss/Mikva bill'?"

In 1975, Representatives Moss and Mikva introduced legislation that favored franchisees more than franchisors. Representatives from all major franchises had been lobbying Congress heavily for more than a year in support of the law.

"We had representatives up in Washington, standing up, yelling and shouting about how terrible Heublein treated everybody and all the things that franchisors were doing," Neal recalled. "Heublein was also getting 'nasty grams' from McDonald's, Burger King, Coke, Pepsi, all the car dealers, the IFA, and the National Franchisor Association. Heublein's stock was probably at a low point in '76, it was fifteen to eighteen dollars a share down from thirty or forty dollars. Things just weren't going well."

In the face of KFC's powerful, independent-minded franchisees, Heublein finally acceded to their demands, and the KFC contract became the model for the industry.

Although the contract had been settled to everyone's satisfaction, Heublein was still suffering. Throughout much of the 1970s (and later into the 1980s), Harman Management simply did not receive much by way of leadership or new product ideas from Heublein and later owners.

"Consequently, Pete was just brilliant in coming up with new ideas for building business during this time," Jackie Trujillo said. "For example, he got a contract with Flavor Pak for corn on the cob and created one of our most popular lunch specials, 'Chicken 'n' Corn.' It included two pieces of chicken, a piece of corn, with mashed potatoes and gravy for just one dollar.

> *"Retail success is not achieved through one masterstroke, but through the relentless attention to a million details . . . all resulting in a satisfactory experience for our customer."*
>
> —James H. Wille

"Following that, he devised what we called our 'Brown Bagger.' This consisted of two pieces of chicken plus a biscuit for ninety-nine cents. Harman's was basically keeping everything alive for building business. We really did not have a big lunch business up until Pete came up with the innovative ideas." Alas, for Kentucky Fried Chicken at large, that innovation was still sadly lacking.

Enter Mike Miles

With the financial slump continuing for Kentucky Fried Chicken, Heublein appointed Mike Miles to chair the ailing division in January 1977. Richard Mayer, who had been vice president of marketing and strategic planning for Heublein's grocery products division, also was named to head KFC's U.S. division.

Miles found a company where product ratings and standards were inconsistent at best, service time was variable, the buildings were old, and only a few had indoor seating facilities. KFC was declining at a compounded rate of 8 percent a year.

It was soon apparent that Miles possessed that rarest of all commodities in corporate management—the ability to see the big picture. He had shown that quality in a previous stint with KFC and was highly regarded in his Heublein executive position.

"In very late 1976," Miles said, "one of the guys that Heublein had running the business called me up and said, 'This thing is going to go in the tank. There's nothing we can do to save it.' At that point I went over and said to the CEO of Heublein, 'You can't let this thing go in the tank. If you've got management down there that thinks it's going to go in the tank, they're not the right people. You better get somebody else.'

"About two weeks later he called me up and said, 'You know what? You're right—and you're that somebody else.' That's how I ended up at Kentucky Fried Chicken the second time.

"What I did know was that the guys who were running it didn't have a clue, although I was so young and so naïve that I wasn't 100 percent sure I could save it—but I never thought of the career risk of not doing it."

Shortly after Miles' assignment was announced publicly, he received a call from Pete Harman asking him to come to Salt Lake City—the sooner the better.

"So one evening in late January, I flew out and was met at the airport by Pete and Einar Bergstedt, his right-hand man," Miles recalled. "There followed for about the next twenty-four hours one of the most intensive motivational experiences that any human being has ever survived—the kind of experience on which Pete's success is built, and for which he is justly famous.

"First, it was to a small room in the Hotel Utah for what we would have called in my college days a 'hotbox session,' with the very simple but effective theme of, 'You can do it, Mike!'" Miles recalled. "Then, after letting me get a couple of hours of sleep, it was up early for a tour of Pete's KFC stores in Salt Lake. This included an item-by-item refresher course on how to do chicken, and examples of the importance of people and motivation—the success in our business.

"We rolled into the airport at 4:26 for me to catch my 4:30 flight back to Louisville. Pete, whose energy level is legendary, leaped out of the car, gave me a hearty poke in the shoulder and in effect ordered me, 'Now Mike, go back there and fix it!'"

> *"See that the people who work with you are recognized for their successes. They'll like you better and work better if you do."*
> —Pete Harman

Among the numerous incentive plans and bonuses Harman had instituted was one that Miles particularly liked, The Top Ten Awards. Pete had invited the first recipients of these awards (first begun following the 1972–73 fiscal year) to a cocktail party at his home and an awards dinner at the Palo Alto Country Club in California. Each year, more and more manager/relief teams achieved Top Ten status—and the party got bigger. Pete said Miles liked the way the program fostered a friendly competition among Harman Management stores.

Using the Harman model, Miles soon classified into three categories what he found at Kentucky Fried Chicken:

1. "I found a company operation system that had taken its eye completely off the ball, that had tried to do a number of different quick fixes, that had cut back on supervision and quality control with the result that the company operation system was really in very deep trouble."
2. "I found a franchise system that, while they had great loyalty to the concept of Kentucky Fried Chicken, were completely disgusted with the company for its lack of leadership and the poor performance in company stores."
3. "And I found that Colonel Sanders was completely alienated from the organization and, as a result of that, was not our goodwill ambassador, as specified in his contract, but was our bad-will ambassador."

Perhaps the gravy didn't actually taste like "wallpaper paste," but Miles believed that the Colonel's observations had merit. "The Colonel was a very independent spirit and rightly observed that the company wasn't doing what it needed to do to maintain his legacy or be successful with his concept, and so he was disgusted," Miles said.

Miles' first step was to meet with Pete Harman and several of the other major franchisees. His second step was to yank a number of ill-chosen new products out of the company store system. Third, he reorganized the aforementioned store supervision. He brought back Jim Wille and put him in charge of company store operations, then refined Richard Mayer's role so that he oversaw marketing. Finally, he named a new chief financial officer, Ed Chambers, and put him in charge of finance and administration.

"We set about to do the very best we possibly could, recognizing that the physical facilities we had were so out of date and in such bad repair, that we weren't going to be able to effect a complete turnaround without new facilities," Miles said. "But we also knew that in order to get the parent company to invest in new facilities at the level that was required, we had to demonstrate some vitality in the system."

Miles then began an exhaustive series of meetings with the franchisees and said, "Look, you've got a lot of legitimate complaints"—one of which was that the company, having promised that it would stop the business of selling equipment and supplies to franchisees at a significant markup, kept right on doing it. Miles took care of that immediately.

"I started going to franchisee meetings and offering myself for open questions and answers on any subject they wanted to talk about or complain about. I talked to them one-on-one about the fact that I was there to do things differently."

And finally, Miles asked for a meeting with the Colonel. "I simply said, 'Hey Colonel, you're absolutely right. Things have been bad, and we're going to make them better.' Then I tried to deliver on that in a way that made the Colonel feel good without making the Colonel feel like he was still in charge of the business—because he wasn't."

The Arrival of QSCVFOOFAMP

Change can be difficult in any corporation, particularly one as large as KFC. Miles worked steadily at his various goals until the changes reached critical mass. If there was a defining moment that marked the company's turnaround, it came at the convention early in Miles' tenure when he introduced the theme of QSCVFOOFAMP—Quality, Service, Cleanliness, Value, Facilities, Other Operating Factors, Advertising, Merchandising, and Promotion.

"QSCVFOOFAMP was a concept that was just beginning to emerge back in those days, which I didn't really know about until later when it was called Total Quality Management," Miles said. "What that meant was that you wouldn't really count on quality improvements being effective for a business if they were only in one aspect of the business. It's still a mystery to too many American corporations today, if I may say so.

"The notion really was to bring KFC back to basics, to throw out all the gimmickry and the over-reliance on price promotion and new products and so on, to take it back to the original recipe chicken."

At one point before Miles' arrival, a number of the company's operating people and franchisees began to say to themselves, "Wait a second. What's wrong here is that people in my area don't like this kind of chicken" and began to tinker with the Colonel's sacred recipe. In most cases, Miles believes that they were making the chicken wrong in the first place. But the knee-jerk reaction was that their problem wasn't their own cooking—it was the recipe.

"We had to put a stop to that," Miles said, "which we did. But the turnaround, the thing that was a critical factor was the new store design, the upgrade of the facilities. We were able to get Heublein to make an investment in the upgrade of facilities because of the fact that the QSCVFOOFAMP operation did demonstrate that there was vitality in the business.

"The first market that we went to with the new stores was Columbus, Ohio. Once the new store design was installed, it turned around and took off. Later, it was just a matter of them maintaining the improvements that we had made in the basic operations, but then rolling out the new store design.

"I think we ended up having something like 112 or 118 straight weeks in succession of sales increases over a year ago in the company stores. And gradually, as the company stores began to improve and show consistent improvement, and as the program of openness and candor with the franchisees proceeded, most of the franchise system began to follow the company's lead on things."

Twenty years later, John Cox still marvels at Miles' gutsy, insightful moves.

"He is smarter than anything," Cox said. "He is brilliant. He is one of the best speakers I have ever heard. When he got up and made a presentation, he was mesmerizing. He decided he needed the Colonel on his side, and QSCVFOOFAMP was right up the Colonel's alley. They marched arm and arm. The Colonel knew he wasn't really running the company anymore, but he knew he was helping drive it in the direction it should go. It took about a year to turn it around. During that period,

Heublein would have sold the company if they could have found somebody to buy it."

Secrets to Success

KFC had several advantages over most corporations hitting rocky shoals. First, if the Colonel's chicken was properly prepared, it was a superior product. Second, the sheer size of Kentucky Fried Chicken meant that there always was significant cash flow. And the third advantage, Miles said, was that KFC had Pete Harman.

"Through it all, people like Pete Harman and other franchisees that had struck pretty close to the way things needed to be done were doing fine," Miles said. "So we knew that there was nothing fundamentally wrong with the concept. We tried to do as many of the things that Pete was doing as we could.

"But I don't want you to think it was easy—easy it wasn't."

Within a couple of years, magazines like *Institutions* were putting Miles on the cover with headlines like "The Spectacular KFC Turnaround."

The "re-colonelization" of Kentucky Fried Chicken had begun.

And the Colonel was very, very happy indeed.

8

The Death of Harland David Sanders

When it became clear that the old warrior was coming to the end of his days, Colonel Sanders had a terse message for his long-time friends at KFC: *Don't close the restaurants!* He couldn't bear the thought of someone not enjoying his beloved chicken just because he died.

KFC was not a business to Harland Sanders—it was an extended family. His legacy was to treat every store as his own. Its problems were his problems. Its successes were his successes. He remained KFC's greatest goodwill ambassador to his final hours.

In the end, the Colonel's personal charge to all KFC employees and franchisees was to continue in the dogged pursuit of excellence. But rather than some esoteric, unattainable ideal, the Colonel's quest for excellence could be summarized in a single concept, a concept that ultimately derived from a time when he had a single restaurant in a converted gasoline station on a dusty road in rural Kentucky.

> *"Run each restaurant like it's your only one."*
> —Harland Sanders

And within that simple statement is a complex business plan that is just as applicable today as it was when he first articulated the concept.

The years that followed, spurred by the turnaround under Mike Miles, were among the happiest of the Colonel's life. Despite several nagging physical conditions, he threw himself into the role of goodwill ambassador for Kentucky Fried Chicken, making commercials, appearing on television, cutting LPs (including *The Colonel's Mandolin Band* and a popular Christmas album), visiting restaurants and, of course, traveling the world.

> *"One of the things that kept me going in those days was the conviction that my Kentucky fried chicken was good— that it was good for the restaurant owner and daggone good for the people who ate it."*
> —Harland Sanders

In the late 1970s, the Colonel began to feel an urgency about visiting old friends. Perhaps he had some inner sense that his time was drawing to a close. In very short order, he managed to drop in on or call numerous long-time franchisees and business associates.

But according to Shirley Topmiller, he found more reasons and excuses to see Pete Harman than anyone else.

"He and Pete Harman have some remarkable similarities," she said. "Pete never once said he had a bad day. Pete started with nothing. Of course, Pete kind of looked at him as the father he never had. He loved the Colonel.

"Or maybe they were more like brothers, because when they were together they were always bumping shoulders, like guys do.

"Pete had the same propensity for recognizing his people. The Colonel liked that. Pete's newsletters were so interesting.

It was all, 'Mary at store 21 had a baby' or 'Rafael and Maria in store 87 got married.' It was all about 'we are family' and this is what we honor and recognize.

"And the Colonel just had this gleeful look when he was with Pete. It was like they shared something that others couldn't get in on."

But as the Colonel aged, Heublein insisted that he employ the use of drivers who also served as bodyguard, guide, and butler as well as chauffeur. His most loyal traveling companion for more than a decade was a tall young man named Dick Miller.

The Dick Miller Decade

In late 1970, twenty-one-year-old Dick Miller, who was working for a carpet store in Shelbyville, went to the Claudia Sanders Dinner House for fried chicken. When he noticed that the yard hadn't been mowed, he sought out the Colonel, who was puttering around the house. Although the Colonel already had a yardman, the two struck up a conversation. The Colonel knew Miller's grandfather.

A few days later, the Colonel's secretary, Maurine McGuire, called Miller at home and asked if he could visit the Colonel on Friday morning. Miller agreed and showed up early. The Colonel outlined his itinerary for the week, the yard work that needed to be done, and then took Miller to the restaurant.

"The Colonel said, 'I'm going to teach you the restaurant business.'"

"I thought, "All of this in a weekend?"

"He said, 'I want you to travel with me. I go all over the world. I'm gone usually twenty or twenty-five days out of the month. They try to get me home every weekend. I need a travel companion.'

"I thought, 'Wow! Do I really want to do this or not?'"

Miller met first with his fiancée, then with Bob Montgomery, the Colonel's first driver. Montgomery eventually became president of the Bank of Birmingham. Montgomery smiled and told Miller, "You'll get along with him if you never tell him no."

Thus began the most memorable ten years of Miller's life, working seven days a week, with no days off, no holidays, no weekends, for one of the most recognizable men in the world. The two averaged more than a quarter of a million miles a year, traveling the world together until the year before the Colonel's death.

According to Miller, the Colonel's colorful past was the origin of another one of his many quirks. Once, as a young man, he'd survived a serious automobile wreck. And, despite the blood, mud, and torn clothing, an executive of Standard Oil mercifully gave him a ride to town. Consequently, the Colonel vowed never to pass a hitchhiker. And he didn't.

"So, when we were driving," Miller recalled, "if you were a hitchhiker, no matter how rough you looked, on the interstate or anywhere, if we come up to you, we'll stop and pick you up.

"Eventually, I talked to John Cox about it. I said, 'We pick up total strangers, some really shady-looking people sometimes, and the Colonel will not let me pass them up.'

> *"I may not always be right, but I'm the boss. And I take full responsibility for anything I tell you to do."*
> —Colonel Sanders

"But when they tried to tell the Colonel it's not safe, the Colonel basically told them where to go—that they weren't going to stop us. Then he chewed me out for going to the company to tell them what was going on. He said, 'What we do in that car *stays* in that car. It has nothing to do with the damn company.'"

"I was privileged to hear a lot of company talk, a lot of recipe talk in the car, but what was said in the car *stayed* in the car."

Through the early- to mid-1970s, most of what Miller heard was the Colonel venting his frustration with Heublein. "People sent letters," Miller said. "Not just to Louisville, these went to the Colonel's home address. So he got to see some of the raw, ticked-off customers. They asked, 'Why did you change the secret recipe?' This was his baby. *He* was the one that put the pots in the back of his car, *he* was the one that slept in his car, *he* was the one that had Claudia drag him all over Hell's Half Acre. He got the thing started; it was a proven thing. And now this company was destroying it. Now he was wishing—and Claudia was wishing—that he hadn't sold it.

"He was really obsessed with at least trying to keep the franchisees controlled. He wanted them to back him up, to help him fight the company because the company kept changing so much. They (Heublein) wanted to do everything, you name it—they wanted fish, they wanted hamburgers, and they wanted to change the cooker. When you can make milk gravy up in Canada, why can't they do it in the U.S.?"

But Heublein's most ill-advised marketing decision had been to downplay the Colonel in KFC advertising. According to Miller, the Colonel's response was vehement—if predictable. "When we would get away from people," Miller said, "the Colonel would voice his opinion in the car: 'These SOBs, they don't realize that they're destroying a good thing.'"

"Re-Colonelization" and the Colonel

Mike Miles and "re-colonelization" changed all that. And Miller's job suddenly got a whole lot easier. The Colonel was, once again, a goodwill ambassador for a company that cherished him.

"I saw airports, hotels, KFC stores, TV studios, radio studios, and company employee picnics," Miller said. "The Colonel enjoyed it because he could get in the car, tune everybody out, and get what they call now a 'power nap.' They used to call them catnaps. He could be in the middle of a sentence, drop his head, be dead asleep for ten or fifteen minutes, wake up, and pick up from that sentence. He rode in the front seat all the time, talking to the people in the back. When they realized he'd dropped off to sleep, they stopped talking to him. And then when he'd wake up again, he'd pick up right where he left off."

The Colonel's reconciliation also meant that he once again returned to KFC's Louisville offices on a regular basis, much to the delight of the employees at The Whitehouse. "He thought everyone around here was his," Shirley Topmiller recalled. "He referred to them as 'the boys and girls.' He knew we were all working for the same thing, and he loved it. He referred to the restaurant employees as 'the boys and girls on the front line.' He felt like they were in the trenches, so to speak, and he knew what they were doing every day, what they were dealing with."

The Colonel kept his ground-floor office at The Whitehouse, though most of the KFC executives were on the second floor. Topmiller said she often accompanied him on his trips to the executive office suite:

"When the elevator would stop on the second floor, where the executive offices were, he would take that cane and put it across everyone in the elevator and say, 'You don't want to get off here, you'll only get in trouble if you get off here.'"

> *"Money isn't everything. I was more interested in doing good and helping people. Like the Rotary Club said, 'Service before Self'."*
>
> —Colonel Sanders

The Final Days

But slowly, that most implacable of all enemies—time—began to catch up with the Colonel. He, of course, refused to recognize his foe and went about business as usual. In fact, the Colonel was nearly eighty-nine when he returned from a globe-spanning tour, one that took him from the Middle East to the Far East.

"He was in Iran just before the Shah got deposed," John Cox recalled with a hint of awe in his voice. "He was over there because people were pirating our trademark and selling Iranian fried chicken. We got a court order, but there was no law left anymore. He went on from there to Japan and came back home. Wasn't feeling well, and went to see a doctor. It was leukemia."

"Toward the end, we pulled into the driveway—we had just come from the Louisville office," Dick Miller recalls.

 ## The Death of Harland David Sanders

"I'm tired. I just hope the franchisees keep doing it as right as possible. I'm ready to go home. I've been here long enough, and I'm ready to quit."

—Harland Sanders

Those who knew the Colonel best said it was clear that the old warrior was wearing down rapidly. In addition to the leukemia and the frequent bouts with pneumonia, he had developed cataracts, diabetes, and severe arthritis. He'd chosen his burial plot in 1973, in Louisville's handsome Cave Hill cemetery. It was said that he chose Louisville over Corbin for his burial because, as one biographer wrote, "he was taking no chances on being stuck away somewhere and forgotten."

In 1980, as he approached ninety, the Colonel had a premonition of his death. He began to put his estate in order, systematically giving away much of his fortune. He began to visit Cave Hill regularly, even as his visits to KFC headquarters dwindled. And, during Kentucky Derby week, he visited his old nemesis, Kentucky's new governor, John Y. Brown, and the governor's new wife, Phyllis George Brown. He even appeared at one last KFC convention in Las Vegas—flatly refusing to follow doctor's orders limiting his hours on the floor with his adoring public.

He was hospitalized in June 1980 and began a strict regimen of chemotherapy. He eventually returned home and made plans to attend his gala ninetieth birthday party celebration in Louisville. But on June 30, he developed pneumonia and was hospitalized again. A second round of chemotherapy had promising results. Still, each trip to the hospital brought new concern—and a new outpouring of love from friends and franchisees across the globe.

The Colonel's birthday party that year in Louisville was one of the largest the city had ever seen. The Riverfront Belvedere's three-day bluegrass festival was transformed into a non-stop party site. The Colonel made a triumphant appearance. And, more importantly, over the weekend KFC stores across the country raised $625,000 towards his favorite charity, the March of Dimes.

Thus began a surreal two months where the Colonel operated as if nothing were wrong—save for his twice-weekly trips to Louisville for chemotherapy. And one of his regular stops was still The Whitehouse in Louisville.

"We still ordered a dozen suits," Topmiller said. "We always ordered the white suits, twelve at a time, from a tailor in Canada. They were British worsted wool, and I still ordered the suits because I thought he'd wear every one of them."

The Colonel's next trip to the hospital was his last. He hung on for weeks, battling leukemia, griping about the food, calling old friends. Claudia and his daughters Margaret and Mildred took turns sitting with him, sometimes talking about the old days, sometimes just sitting in silence. In the end, even his memory failed.

"I didn't want to see him like that," Topmiller said. "One day someone came in the office and said, 'I think the Colonel is a little better.' I left the building and went to see him. He called me by the wrong name—but he knew. He stopped himself, but he couldn't pull it forward. Later someone said, 'You should have said your name.' But I just couldn't. I finally decided, 'I'm not going to go back.'"

But the reports by December 15 were noticeably less optimistic, and when the nurse checked his pulse at 7:45 on the morning of December 16, Harland David Sanders was dead. Despite John Cox's best efforts to make sure that KFC employees were the first to know, Shirley Topmiller, Dick Miller, and most of the employees at The Whitehouse heard the news on their way to work that morning.

Because of the deep affection most of the employees felt for the old Colonel, Topmiller insisted that the body should lie in state at KFC headquarters, and Cox eventually agreed.

"I thought the employees should be the first to see him after the family," she recalled, "so his body was brought to The Whitehouse and he lay in state here.

"After the coffin was placed, they announced to the employees that you could pass by it and to leave for the day. Then the public was invited to come, and that went on until late, late that night. People just came and came and came. And, of course, some franchisees were arriving by then, too. It was lovely, it was just so lovely."

Almost immediately after the official announcement, Cox said he heard from Governor Brown.

"John Y. wanted to have him lie in state at the rotunda over in the state capitol in Frankfurt, which of course was not in my plan," Cox said. "I asked Claudia, 'What do you want to do?' She thought that would be all right, so that's what we did."

During a memorial service at the rotunda, Brown told the uncommonly quiet audience about the mark the Colonel had made on him—and a million others as well.

At the close of the service, while "My Old Kentucky Home" was sung, Brown and Claudia Sanders placed a state flag on the coffin. The funeral service was held at Southern Baptist Theological Seminary. At the request of the family, Dick Miller drove the hearse to the Alumni Chapel. Despite the bitter cold, long rows of Boy Scouts lined the streets as an honor guard. The Scouts had always been one of the Colonel's favorite charities.

Among the first to arrive had been Pete Harman and a large contingent from Harman Management. Pete sat close to the grieving family. "He belonged to the whole nation," Harman said. "You don't replace someone like that. You can't."

"The music was by Pat Boone," Topmiller recalled. "The Colonel loved listening to Pat Boone. Boone and the Colonel had been on the dais together one Easter Sunday years ago, and the Colonel never forgot that. He had always said to me, 'I'd like to have Pat Boone sing at my funeral.'"

Boone sang "What a Friend We Have in Jesus" and "He Touched Me."

Press coverage of the funeral services was worldwide and almost uniformly sympathetic. Among the most insightful of the tributes was an editorial in *The Louisville Courier-Journal*:

"The story of the Colonel's repeated triumphs over adversity, of the warm heart inside the crusty exterior, and of his final emergence as a global legend at an age when most folks have long since retired, is familiar. Indeed, one of the consolations of his death yesterday was that the world had so fully recognized its debt and graced his final years with well-deserved tributes and honors."

Remembering the Colonel

John Cox, KFC's masterful public relations director during the difficult years of Heublein's initial relationship with the Colonel, found himself at a loss for words when asked to measure the Colonel's impact—more than twenty years after his passing. At last, after considering his initial response for more than a week, he penned the following tribute:

"The Colonel was a catalyst in changing the way the world eats. He was, if not *the* father, then *one of* the fathers of fast food.

"His timing was perfect—although entirely accidental. He—or more accurately, his surrogates the franchisees—provided wholesome, tasty, affordable take-out meals at a time when women were entering the workforce in increasing numbers and needed someone to cook supper for them occasionally.

> *"The Colonel belonged among the finest men who ever called Kentucky home. I can hardly think of a single person who's had a greater impact on more people than Colonel Sanders."*
> —John Y. Brown

"The Colonel didn't invent take-out. His franchisees did. He'd thought of his chicken as an entrée item on a restaurant menu. But the franchisees—notably Pete Harman—found it to be the perfect take-out meal. The bone helped keep the chicken hot on the trip from the store to the home.

"In the field of advertising, the Colonel started another trend—the founder or CEO as spokesman, guaranteeing the quality of the product. We see it today with Dave Thomas, who was a KFC franchisee before he founded Wendy's. Dave and the Colonel were good friends.

"The Colonel was a great trademark and a spokesman. He radiated integrity and honesty, as Dave Thomas still does. You just knew that the Colonel wouldn't lie to you, that he wouldn't cheat you, that he had a good product.

"My guess is that, even at the peak of his fame, most consumers thought he came from Central Casting," Cox added. "He was just too good to be real. At one point, he was one of the most recognized people in the world. He probably still is, although most people may think he's the brainchild of some marketing whiz. A Ronald McDonald or a Jolly Green Giant in mufti.

"But he was a very real man, a hard-working poor guy from Indiana who pulled himself up by his bootstraps. Repeatedly. His life was a series of failures. If he'd died at age sixty-five, the world would not have noticed. Or if it had, he'd have been judged a fail-

> "He was a memorable man, a simple man, an interesting man, frequently an irritating man—and one helluva cook."
> —John Cox

ure. He had little education. No rich friends. His secret—besides the eleven herbs and spices—was that he never quit.

"He was a success in spite of himself. His ego was as large as it was fragile. He had a hair-trigger temper. He was profane, although by today's standards he didn't have a foul mouth. He didn't always recognize who his friends were. (The Colonel felt a great animosity toward John Y. Brown, who truly was the Colonel's friend.) The Colonel was a lousy businessman. He made a great many people very wealthy, but he gave away virtually all of his money. He had a good heart and was a sucker for anybody with a sob story. He also hated paying taxes."

Equally revealing are the comments of Dave Thomas, chairman of Wendy's International, in the days following the Colonel's death:

"The Colonel really wasn't a restaurant guy in the strictest sense. Many of his franchisees were more successful operators. And he wasn't the best businessman, either; he never planned for the future; never was a good organization man.

"But he did things the best businessman couldn't do. He was one of the world's greatest salesmen. He knew how to get

> *"The Colonel had that magic of making people succeed, probably beyond their natural capacity. Everybody respected him. They wanted to succeed for him as much as for themselves."*
> —Pete Harman

along with people. He was dynamite on quality, and he developed an esprit de corps among franchisees that was fantastic.

"Kentucky Fried Chicken was a family situation. He would send new franchisees to me in Columbus, Ohio, to explain the system, and franchisees were always helping each other out. Most even showed their books to each other. That was unheard of in the restaurant business."

Mike Miles said, "The Colonel was a perfectionist, and when he didn't get the quality he demanded, he'd pound his cane on the table, and things would get better. In recent years, he had not found it necessary to bang his cane as often, which pleased him greatly.

"Our Colonel is no longer around to bang his cane. But if we settle for less than he would have, we will squander his legacy and besmirch his memory.

"We have not lost the Colonel as long as we remember to do things right. Each of us must take up the Colonel's cane."

An Era of Change, Growth

The years that followed the Colonel's death were a tumultuous time in the history of KFC. Guided by Mike Miles's emphasis on the "re-colonelization" of the brand, KFC grew once again. The company expanded rapidly abroad and soon became a prime acquisition target, passing first to R.J. Reynolds and ultimately to corporate giant PepsiCo, which brought enormous reserves of cash and talent to KFC, along with special challenges.

Through it all, savvy operators continued to remember Miles's prophetic words—"Nothing in the restaurant business is ever permanently fixed, or ever permanently broken."

The end result was that the lessons learned in previous years—*Success is in the details . . . Every penny counts . . .* and *If you lose quality, you lose it all*—enabled them to prevail regardless of the circumstances. Encapsulated into a single concept, this perseverance became stated as follows:

The customer's opinion is what counts.

It was an important lesson during an exciting time.

"It is no exaggeration to say that while there would be no KFC as we know it without the Colonel, there would also be no KFC as we know it without Pete Harman."
—Mike Miles

KFC's Secret Weapon

If others worried that the death of Kentucky Fried Chicken's founder, spokesman, and icon would have a damaging effect on KFC, Mike Miles would have none of it. At a banquet honoring Pete Harman's forty years in the business, Miles happily claimed that Pete was KFC's "secret weapon."

"Pete helps to oversee all this as a member of the Heublein board of directors. And while his purview as a director includes the full range of our businesses, his first love continues to be KFC, and his participation and assistance in the management of the KFC system is intensive," Miles said.

"But as large and far-flung as the system is, Pete is closely involved in all aspects of it. I suspect that seldom a day goes by without Pete being on the phone with someone, somewhere in our organization, answering a question, giving advice, lending encouragement, or adding a sense of urgency."

Miles told the banquet audience that Harman's sales had always been among the highest in the entire KFC system. "And because Pete understands motivation better than anyone I have ever known, except perhaps the Colonel, it shouldn't be surprising that by simply holding out his own high sales levels as a target, he can inspire others to a high level of enthusiasm to catch him and match him. He is, following the passing of the Colonel, now clearly the personal symbol of our system."

The death of the Colonel only temporarily obscured the job Mike Miles, with Dick Mayer, had done in righting KFC's listing ship. *Institutions* magazine's cover story for December 1980 trumpeted "The Spectacular KFC Turnaround" and featured Miles on the cover. Miles, as was his custom, was cautious, telling the magazine, "Nothing in the restaurant business is ever permanently fixed, or ever permanently broken."

But compared with the dismal days of 1976–77, when KFC profits dropped dramatically—and KFC was counted on to generate at least a quarter of Heublein's profits—the company's turnaround had been little short of amazing. "This was no simple problem," Miles said. "I couldn't help feeling at the time that cracking the atom would be quite a bit simpler."

But with the help of a top-flight management team, operators Pete Harman, John R. Neal, Jim Collins, and other loyal franchisees, Miles admitted he'd finally discovered how to smash that atom.

"At the end of the day, the reason people go to quick-service restaurants is for good food, quick service, and good value," he said. "Basically, what we did was try to give people what we knew they wanted. One of the things that made it survive was that our research showed that although the customers weren't satisfied, they were more than willing to give it another chance because in many cases KFC was the closest place to their house. Their kids remembered it and liked it.

"The other reason we knew it would likely work is because people like Pete Harman and Jim Collins and other franchisees who had stuck pretty close to the way things needed to be done were doing fine. So we knew that there was nothing fundamentally wrong with the concept. We tried to do as many of the other things that Pete was doing as we could."

Getting Down to Business

John R. Neal still speaks admiringly of Mike Miles and his style of leadership more than twenty-five years later:

"Mike was the kind of guy who'd say, 'Let's cut out the BS. Let's get down to business. Tell me if my breath smells bad or I'm naked or you don't like what's going on. Let's figure out how to fix it together.' That was the kind of guy he was. If Mike told you something, he would *do* it."

His staff felt much the same way. Donald E. Parkinson, who joined KFC in May 1980 from General Motors, said his first meeting with Miles set the tone for their subsequent relationship:

"I was sitting there talking to Mike, and he had a bowl of mashed potatoes and gravy in front of him. He said, 'The Colonel says our gravy tastes like wallpaper paste. That's what he said on *Johnny Carson*. We're making progress, but we're still not there. It may seem strange to you to see me eating mashed potatoes and gravy at three in the afternoon, but that's our life here.'"

Although Miles ultimately mirrored much of what Pete Harman had been preaching all along, Pete refused to say "I told you so" to the other members of Heublein's board. Instead, according to Jim Olson—by then an area consultant—he continued with the original philosophy that had made him a millionaire many times over: "It's not about chicken. It's about people."

"Pete is not the most analytical person I know," Olson said. "I've asked him several times, 'Pete, when you started out did you ever think you would have three hundred stores?' He'd say, 'No.' 'When you moved to California, was that a goal of yours?' 'No.'

"When you ask him anything about himself, it was never a long-term plan of his to accomplish anything. I think he's broken his life up into smaller segments and just made decisions as he went."

"On another side, I was with him on a business deal where we were trying to buy a piece of property in San Rafael," Olson recalled. "It took a long time to get hold of the gentleman who was actually on the board of directors for the large company that owned this piece of land. We drove around with the man, who kept saying he didn't want to sell it.

"Meanwhile, Pete was telling him old stories about the Colonel and schmoozing him. Finally, Pete said, 'Pull over in the lot here.' So we pulled over on a piece of dirt. I sat in the front seat with Pete, while the gentleman in question was in the back seat.

"Pete turned around and said, 'You've got about fifteen more days before you've got to file your fourth-quarter earnings statement, and you know it's not going to look very good. About $800,000 cash for this piece of dirt would probably make it look a little better.'

"This guy's face just went blank. He didn't respond, but we kept talking, and then we decided to go to dinner. At dinner we talked a while and, at last, Pete said, 'Well, are you going to go back to New York with some money or aren't you?'

"And the guy said, 'Yes.'

"So Pete went to the restroom.

"The gentleman turned to me and said, 'Who *is* this guy?'

"I said, 'What do you mean?'

"He says, 'Well, he's either a country bumpkin or the smartest SOB ever.'

"My answer was, 'He's both. He is who he is.'

"But Pete had done his research. He knew who he was going up against and knew he had to talk tough with this guy to do the deal."

The rest of KFC was prospering just as Harman's was prospering. By 1981, Heublein had seen enough progress from Miles's back-to-basics approach to invest $35 million in renovation of the company stores and their original red-and-white striped buildings. The investment paid off handsomely in a relatively short time.

But Miles wanted Heublein to invest in the franchisees as well, figuring it would take both groups to create a true turnaround. According to John R. Neal, then president of the Southeastern Association (the largest of the regional franchisee associations), the franchisees were just as eager for some assistance in remodeling their stores. Eventually, the two men met in Atlanta to work something out. Neal said Miles approached the meeting with his typically direct style:

"Mike said, 'John R., we've got a huge problem here. We have got to reinvest our assets. We've got to fix these chicken stores. We've got to upgrade them. What are we going to do? How do we go about getting franchisees to do that?'"

Neal said he was ready for just such a question. He cited the new Investment Tax Credit, a law that had been enacted to stimulate the weak economy of 1978. According to Neal, if a business made an investment, then the government gave that business 10 percent credit against their taxes. The ITC was designed to spur investment at a time when money was tight and interest rates were high.

Neal suggested that the franchisee make the initial investment.

"Make him show that if he spends forty, fifty, or sixty thousand bucks in his store, whatever that number happens to be, you'll give him a 10 percent credit. Let him abut it against his royalties and pay him out over three years. That way you can control the amount of money you give back based on the investment *and* you can control the payout on it. Because if a franchisee puts $50,000 to $75,000 in his restaurant, he's going to get a boost in sales, is he not? Isn't that what all the test markets have shown? So you're going to get a staggered higher royalty two or three years down the road. They don't need it all in one year, but you give them something and they'll go for it."

> *"If you want to get someone to invest, invest in them."*
> —Pete Harman

In Neal's account of the meeting, the two men fine-tuned the plan and eventually came up with a program that was so successful that KFC extended it two years beyond its original deadline. "It was Mike Miles's incentive program that jump-started the KFC sales and system," Neal said. "Once the corporation began to put money in their restaurants, sales increased, and we were off and running." Franchisee and company stores alike received a further boost with Miles and Mayer's highly successful 1981 ad campaign, "We Do Chicken Right."

> *"A rising tide raises all boats."*
> —John F. Kennedy

International Growth

By 1982, KFC had become Heublein's fastest-growing division, with real growth of 2.3 percent. Since 1978, company unit sales had jumped a whopping 73 percent. Franchisee growth also was impressive—almost 45 percent. Admittedly, much of the initial growth came from KFC's burgeoning international operations, where KFC stores now outnumbered McDonald's outlets. The freewheeling international operation flourished in part because individual stores again were allowed to cater to local tastes.

KFC Around the World

➤ Australian consumers preferred rotisserie chicken long before it became available in the United States.

➤ KFC stores in England were swamped after 8:00 PM., as Kentucky Fried Chicken was a popular snack after an evening in the pubs. English-style "chips" replaced mashed potatoes on the menu.

➤ In Guam, KFC customers liberally doused their orders of red rice with Tabasco and soy sauce.

➤ In Japan, most of the stores offered rice and a special kind of smoked chicken in addition to the Colonel's Original Recipe.

The overseas explosion was most impressive along the Pacific Rim. In 1983, Singapore alone was home to twenty-three franchised stores, and Japan boasted nearly four hundred stores. In Japan, Kentucky Fried Chicken employees underwent a Spartan training regimen in a remote mountain camp. During the course of the training session, potential employees endured rigorous physical and psychological workouts to prove that they were "worthy" of a lifetime job with KFC.

Rapid growth in Japan was due, in great part, to the leadership of Takeshi "Shin" Okawara. Okawara was a paper-box salesman in Japan when KFC chose Expo '70 to launch its first store. Loy Weston, KFC's Japanese representative, quickly noticed Okawara's people skills and hired him. The first Kentucky Fried Chicken store opened on November 23, 1970. Two others soon followed.

But after the initial excitement, the three stores soon fell behind their sales projections. Okawara was asked to come to Louisville to study KFC's American operations. Some unknown hero pulled Okawara aside and whispered, "If you want to know about Kentucky Fried Chicken, you have to meet Pete Harman."

After completing the mandatory training course in Louisville, Okawara traveled to Palo Alto. "Pete let me stay at his place," Okawara said, "and Jackie and Einar and the others all trained me. The best part is I got a sense of the Harman ethic, how to think and how to deal with people.

> *"One day I asked Pete, 'What is the essence of the success of this business?' His answer was 'People.' He told me that if you take care of your people, people would take care of you. That's what he said. That is true even now."*
> —Shin Okawara

Once back home, Okawara found that Pete's philosophy was eagerly accepted by KFC's Japanese employees. "I tried his philosophy exactly as Pete taught me," Okawara recalled. "I really took care of my people and my people really took care of me. At the same time, he told me of the importance of customer relations and the quality of the operations. I'm proud that I'm an operations guy, not a strategic or financial guy. I'm the operations guy." Soon, sales skyrocketed, and Japan became one of the jewels in KFC's crown. Okawara quickly became "Mr. Japan" at KFC.

"Each year I realize and appreciate Pete's advice and what I got from Pete Harman's family," he said. "For me, he is really a good father.

"In those days in Japan, business was booming, and everybody tended to forget about the people aspect. But we at KFC-Japan never forgot about the fact that we are the family, we are the people-oriented company. With the economy going down the tubes, we are still doing great. I think that is because of the family-oriented philosophy. Of course, efficiency and business activity practices are very important. But, at the same time, we shouldn't forget about the importance of the people."

Looking for a White Knight

If there was a dark cloud on the horizon for Mike Miles, it was that KFC's growth was limited by the lack of expansion capital at Heublein. Board member Pete Harman said that after the initial investment for refurbishing company stores, Heublein was pumping most of its available cash into trying to stem the losses in its sagging spirits division, which was suffering from flat domestic sales and increased competition. As a result, McDonald's expansion fund in 1982 was eight times the amount allotted to KFC.

According to Harman, the Heublein board of directors also was worried that the company might become the victim of a hostile takeover and have its various components sold in pieces as a result. Corporate stock raider General Cinema already was buying large chunks of Heublein stock and, according to Pete Harman, the Heublein board began looking for a "white knight." They found one in Winston-Salem, North Carolina.

If Heublein was slumping, R.J. Reynolds was not. In an effort to diversify, the tobacco giant had been in an acquisitions mode since the late 1970s. "Reynolds was looking to expand into the consumer products industry so it could use its marketing skills and huge cash flow," Harman said. "Reynolds was very profitable back then, but by 1982 the tobacco side of things was getting hit by higher taxes and just a general decline in smoking. Heublein probably looked pretty good to them."

After a few months of negotiating, R.J. Reynolds purchased Heublein for $1.4 billion. "Unfortunately, there didn't appear to be a place for Mike Miles after the acquisition," Harman said. "I give him a lot of credit for the turnaround. We all hated to see him go." Miles left to become president of Dart and Kraft Foods. He was quickly replaced as CEO of KFC by Richard Mayer.

Twenty years later, the ever-modest Miles still had fond memories of his remarkable tenure as head of KFC. "I do feel pretty good about it. I do want to emphasize—and I don't think I'm any more modest than the next guy—that I had just a terrific group of people to work with. Likewise, among the

R.J. Reynolds Acquisitions

Del Monte (1979)
Canada Dry (1984)
Heublein/KFC (1982)
Sunkist Soft Drinks (1984)
Nabisco Brands (1985)

key franchisees, there were people like Pete and a lot of supporters who were willing to help me work through the initial very difficult relationship with the franchise system as a whole. It was not in any way, shape, or form a one-man show."

But according to Don Parkinson and others, Miles deserved an enormous amount of credit. "If you look back on the Heublein days, you had some people who didn't understand the brand when coming in to run KFC. Not only didn't they understand it, they didn't respect it. They didn't want to learn about it. They just thought it was a brand, so what's the problem? You had some franchisees who were good and some of them were terrible. So you had that rift. You had the good franchisees saying, 'Heublein—we're paying you royalties, where the hell is the leadership?' So you have all of that turmoil going on. Mike reached out and listened to them and not only listened, he acted on some of their recommendations. And he really made that thing work."

Perhaps the old Colonel—who hated cigarettes—would have cringed, but on the surface the acquisition by Reynolds appeared to be a good match.

Harman applauded Reynolds' vision for expansion and its strong international presence. And after the lean years of Heublein, Reynolds' apparently inexhaustible financial reserves were particularly welcome.

"KFC grossed something like $2.4 billion in 1982," Harman said, "and things were really going good. In 1983, we had 4,500 stores in the U.S. and another 1,400 stores in fifty-four foreign countries. Nobody but McDonald's was even close to us."

Smaller franchisees like LaRue Kohl also liked what new owner Reynolds brought to the table. For the first time, a "franchise manager" (FM) began to visit his seven stores on a regular basis. Kohl's FM taught his employees the nuances of "suggestive selling" and conducted training seminars for sales hosts. At the same time, Kohl could see the physical transformation of the nearby company-owned stores.

"I remember thinking, 'We're remodeling restaurants *and* we're remodeling people,'" Kohl recalled.

But Kohl's most vivid memory occurred at a KFC convention shortly after the purchase by R.J. Reynolds. Reynolds took the occasion to honor Pete Harman for his years of loyal service to the company:

"They asked him to say something—after they awarded him the pin in front of everybody at the convention—about the secrets of success in the chicken business. Pete stood up and said, 'You know, "I'm not in the chicken business. I'm in the people business.'

Harman Philosophies

- ▶ **"More opportunities for more people**. The only way you keep doing that is to put people first."
- ▶ **"We've always developed from within**. I think that is a different modus—we don't go out and look for college graduates. A lot of them graduate from college, or go to school and graduate while they're working for us."
- ▶ **"Making people belong**. Let them know you appreciate what they do. I don't particularly want the company to get a lot bigger."
- ▶ **"The magic is working together**—like a great big family."

"This was way before this became a buzz phrase. That really stuck with me. I remember thinking, 'Hey, that's right!' And I started looking for ways to help make our people better. Why that sticks in my mind—because that was the first time we saw corporate folks coming in as a real help to us. R.J. Reynolds really did bring some neat programs."

Like Miles before him, Mayer maintained a close relationship with Harman. Pete said he appreciated Dick's cautious attitude when it came to both corporate policies as well as new products. Even while other magazines were trumpeting KFC's resurgence, Mayer told *Nation's Restaurant News*, "People keep talking about the turnaround at KFC. I'd really rather not talk about it. The turnaround is only halfway over. In the past two years, people have gone absolutely schizoid. A lot of chains have blurred their image by adding so many new menu items. We don't roll out a flavor-of-the-month."

Coping With New Markets

Encouraged by the new partnership with Reynolds, Harman Management continued to expand in the 1980s. It was at this time that it first encountered a different audience base in the new urban markets. And, according to Pete Harman, new markets sometimes call for new approaches.

"We always had been primarily a suburban operation," Harman recalled. "What had worked in suburban Sacramento suddenly wasn't working in inner city Oakland. We had stores that were struggling, and that was a new experience for all of us. It was time to be creative. So I looked to Jim Olson. Jim had been an area consultant by then for five or six years. I wanted him to become a regional director. To do that, I wanted to give him a challenge."

Harman's Challenge List

► To make employees grow, give them a challenge.
► To determine if employees are up to a challenge, give them a challenge.
► To avoid routine, give someone a new challenge.
► To make a business grow, give it a challenge.

The challenge was Oakland, then the lowest performing market in the Harman system.

"I was certainly not somebody that was brought up to be the inner city manager of people," Olson said, "but Pete creates this attitude in your mind that you can do anything. His expectation of you is not perfection but only to do the best that you can do. The line he has repeated to hundreds of people is, 'Just be the best Jim Olson you can be. You don't have to be Pete Harman. You don't have to be Jackie Trujillo. You don't have to be as good as some other guy you think is better than you. Just be the best you can be.' And he sincerely means it."

But Oakland proved to be a tough market to crack, and the transformation took Olson and his team seven hard-fought years. "It took a lot longer than I thought it was going to take," he recalled. " But I wanted a permanent change—not what I call 'lipstick on a pig.' When you're done, you've still got a pig.

"So it took seven years, but we ended up being the number-one region in the company. To do it, I brought in a new product line that was particular to our demographics.

"The main thing we did was to develop people who were from the neighborhoods and wanted to continue living there. We were a pretty lily-white company at that time, and most of our people were out of touch with what a market like San Francisco or

New Products for New Markets
1. *Spicy Chicken*
2. *Mean Greens*
3. *Spicy Rice*
4. *Buttermilk Biscuits*

Oakland was. They came to Oakland for an opportunity to work for a year, do a good job, get the heck out of Dodge, and go into suburbia.

"What took building the area so long was setting an expectation that not only running the store was a part of your job but the development of your people also was part of your job. We graduated from D talent to C to B to finally A talent in Oakland over the years."

The new approach increased volume in Harman's inner city stores by 68 percent. Olson, again, gave Harman much of the credit, claiming that Pete empowered him to move quickly—both on the personnel changes and on implementation of the new menu items.

> *"When Pete acts, he acts quickly. He does things with 100 percent passion and commitment."*
>
> —Jim Olson

"I think that attitude has been taken on by our entire company. When we decide to do something, KFC is often amazed at how quickly we can bring everybody to focus on what the task is and get it done. We've just mimicked Pete in that way. If there is a new idea, we don't send it out to focus groups and sub-committee it to death. We *do* it," Olson added.

Honoring Aunt Carrie

That's the way Pete Harman had learned to operate from his beloved Aunt Carrie. When there was a need or a problem, she responded immediately. It was an object lesson that Pete saw lived out every day while growing up in Granger.

"As I grew older, I began to see even more clearly what an inspiration Aunt Carrie had been to so many people," Harman said. "I wanted somehow to honor that. I'd been kicking around the idea of giving some money to Brigham Young University, but I hadn't really decided on anything specific.

"Finally, someone at the university said they needed a building for their Continuing Education (CE) Division, which is the largest in the world with more than 33,000 enrollments each year. Besides CE courses, they also wanted a place to host the Native American Services and the new Adult Development and Aging divisions—two areas that were close to my heart."

When Harman agreed to donate the money for the building, BYU officials were delighted and decided to name the building for him. But Pete would have none of that. And even though BYU had never named a building for a woman, he insisted that it be called The Caroline Hemenway Harman Building. Brigham Young trustees agreed.

The end result was the most striking building on campus, a mirror-glassed showplace that reflects the sky and surrounding mountains.

At the dedication in the spring of 1982, Gordon B. Hinckley, speaking for the church, said, "There is no other campus that I know of with a building named after a woman who was relatively unknown and unsung, whose accomplishments were not in the professions but in the home, and whose concerns were not with rights but with responsibilities. Her life was characterized by service and by self-reliance, by the attitude 'Somehow we'll do it, by the principles of thrift, honor, integrity, and charity.'"

"Pete's sense of jumping in, I think, was brought on by his Aunt Carrie," Jim Olson observed. "She was such a great role model for him in terms of being a giver and, secondly, always sacrificing herself or her time or her food or whatever it was that she had to give—it automatically went to others. I think Pete modeled himself after his Aunt Carrie, since she was the only parent he had. He became like her."

> *"In the business world, he created that same kind of thing. He kind of 'Aunt Carrie'd' us. He'd put his arm around us and say, 'Just go out and do the best you can.'"*
>
> —Jim Olson

"People draw back from trying when they're afraid of failing. Pete says 'Go out and try this.' You think, 'Jeez, I don't know how to do this.' He says, 'That's okay. Go out and do it.' Only then do you realize that you're *not* going to get in trouble for trying, so your mind opens up and you start thinking about what you *can* do instead of what you can't do," Olson said.

Competitors Multiply

The impact and viability of "The Harman Formula" was rarely more evident than in the early- to mid-1980s. Harman Management stores were enjoying solid, sometimes spectacular growth. Pete's goal for the 1980s was to make 25 percent of his stores "Million Dollar Stores." In 1982, Utah's Millstream reached the million-dollar mark. In 1983, Harman-Wall in San Jose was the first million-dollar take-home. Others soon followed, and KFC's overall success once again spawned a new crop of imitators.

New Kids on the Block, 1982

Church's	Pioneer Takeout
Popeye's	Po' Folks
Bojangles	Tinsley's
Mrs. Winner's	Golden Skillet
Famous Recipe	

Some of the competition was well financed. Famous Recipe was backed by Shoney's, while Golden Skillet was bankrolled by International Dairy Queen. Also firmly established by 1982 was Chick-fil-A, with 240 units—mostly in shopping malls.

Perhaps the most interesting aspect of the new competition was that the founders and CEOs of many of the second generation of chicken restaurants had deep KFC roots. Even Jack Massey, who (along with John Y. Brown) initially purchased Kentucky Fried Chicken from the Colonel, got in the act by developing the Mrs. Winner's chain, originally called Granny's Fried Chicken. In response, Harman said that R.J. Reynolds committed more than $168 million to KFC's expansion plans in 1984 alone.

"Just as important as the money was the nature of Reynolds," Harman said. "They were both highly diversified and highly decentralized, which meant they pretty much left us alone. We were pretty autonomous during this period. It worked pretty well at first."

Dick Mayer concurred. In late April 1984, he told *Restaurant Business* magazine that—in the early days, at least—the KFC/R.J. Reynolds partnership was a business marriage made in heaven. "They seem to want the same things we do, and they are as heavily consumer product-oriented as we are. "We never would have been able to accomplish this degree of growth under Heublein, much less on our own."

According to Harman, Mayer also gradually increased KFC's level and commitment to training. "Dick really pushed a two-tiered program," Pete said. "One side was the STAR system (Store Training and Rating), which we'd started in 1977. The other was CAP (Career Advancement Program), which was first tested in 1981. Both worked out nicely.

"At Harman's we added some things of our own as well, including Ambassadors and the Harman's Best Program, in addition to even more training at probably every level."

Thanks to the increased emphasis on training, turnover dropped dramatically and production increased across the board. In the test markets of Kansas City and Cincinnati, "team member" (hourly employee) turnover dropped from 200 percent to 120 percent in less than a year.

Harman said that Reynolds continued to pump money into KFC in part because they believed that increasingly health-conscious consumers would shift to chicken. To that end, the company outlined a $1 billion expansion plan over five years. "That was great, but the bulk of the money was earmarked for overseas markets, because so many of them were still wide open territories," Harman added.

"It didn't always work out like they wanted. Some of these franchisees owned several different companies, and the local KFC would be just a small part of the pie. Some of these operators milked a market dry, or they would cut corners to make money. I think, in some places anyway, it allowed system integrity to suffer. "Still, some other places, like Japan—which had operators who loved and understood the KFC culture—flourished."

Asian Expansion

Reynold's overseas expansion of KFC franchisees continued through the early 1980s, reaching eighty-five stores in Southeast Asia alone. Harry Schwab later headed up the region, but only after building forty-eight company-owned and ninety-five franchise stores in South Africa alone. "But the most impressive expansion was back into Hong Kong," Harman said. "KFC had been out of Hong Kong for more than a decade, which allowed all of the burger chains to dominate the market. Still, that gave us an educated audience with lots of disposable income—and a taste for American-style foods.

"KFC opened something like twenty stores in Hong Kong. The first store sold more than 40,000 pieces of chicken during its first week—which is still a KFC record. Our success there enabled KFC to begin thinking about the world's biggest untapped market—China."

The growth of the early 1980s meant that even while R.J. Reynolds was spending hundreds of millions in expansion abroad and upgrading company stores, Harman Management and other franchisees were able to generate sufficient income to both renovate existing stores and build new stores using KFC's latest model. The difference was in the speed Harman was able to remodel.

Gross Comparisons, 1983

Average franchisee—$398,000 annually
Average company store—$525,000 annually
Average Harman store—$600,000 annually

Beginning with his two hundredth KFC outlet, in West Valley City (outside Salt Lake City) in August 1984, all of Harman's new stores would be built in KFC's "Heritage" style.

"We're just upgrading our stores and getting rid of the plastic look to make dining more enjoyable," Pete told a local newspaper at the time. He said that every fifth store in the Harman chain would be remodeled in 1984, utilizing the Heritage theme—family-style dining, with a large dining room, oak décor, and a "customer ambassador" attending to each customer's needs.

R.J. Reynolds' own focus on its "image enhancement" campaign meant that by the end of 1984, 93 percent of its

1,126 company stores had been remodeled. Also by the end of 1984, Reynolds had bankrolled KFC's purchase of Gino's master territory in the Northeast (160 restaurants), launched the Mexican-themed Zantigo chain (sixty-one stores), and boosted annual company store sales (or PRA—per restaurant average) to nearly $600,000. In short, it appeared that everybody was happy, domestically and internationally, franchisee and franchisor.

Jim Olson's memory of this period is equally upbeat. "I remember Pete one day going through one of our training meetings and looking around. He finally said, 'How many nationalities do we have here?' We counted them, and we had thirty-one different nationalities in the room. Pete just laughed his head off.

"My interpretation of that laugh was, 'You know, this culture works for everybody. It isn't something that's just a Utah culture. It's something that can work even in the inner-city markets. People are all the same. People want to do better in life, people like to be recognized for their contributions and they still like to be a part of a group. They like being part of something a little bigger than themselves.'

A Fading Honeymoon

In time, however, even the KFC/R.J. Reynolds honeymoon faded. Although he never complained publicly, Pete eventually grew weary of R.J. Reynold's erratic leadership even as Harman Management continued to expand. "Not that they weren't a good company, they just didn't know a lot about the chicken business," he said. "They didn't really care if you were flourishing or not. There were times within KFC that they were doing really well, and then there were times when they didn't do so well. Sometimes the money was there, sometimes it wasn't."

What had begun with Reynolds allowing KFC to prosper with minimal interference eventually evolved into distance and, eventually, indifference. And R.J. Reynolds had changed. It was now RJR Nabisco, Inc., and was going through the throes of a complete reorganization. In mid-1985, rumors began swirling around Louisville and Los Altos that another deal was in the works. Pete Harman and others at KFC believed that there would come a time that RJR Nabisco would decide that a chain of chicken restaurants was not a good fit in its overall portfolio.

PepsiCo, Inc., on the other hand, did.

"We didn't fit," Dick Mayer told *Restaurant & Institutions*. "R.J. Reynolds is a behemoth in the packaged goods business. PepsiCo has a major interest in the restaurant business. It's a better fit. We will get better understanding by PepsiCo of who we are and what we need. They obviously had done their homework. They had tremendous respect and knowledge for the turnaround Kentucky Fried Chicken had gone through." Michael H. Jordan, PepsiCo president, later admitted that PepsiCo had begun initial inquiries about purchasing KFC as early as 1985.

On October 1, 1986, RJR Nabisco sold its restaurants to PepsiCo, Inc. for approximately $840 million.

PepsiCo, a Good Fit

At the time, KFC was the second largest restaurant chain in the world with more than 6,500 stores and sales of nearly $3.5 billion. Unlike Heublein and R.J. Reynolds, PepsiCo did have quick-service restaurant experience. The soft-drink giant had purchased Pizza Hut in 1977 and Taco Bell in 1978. And since the initial merger between Herman Lay's Frito-Lay and Donald Kendall's Pepsi in 1965, PepsiCo had flourished by consistently rolling out new products through all of its divisions.

The ever-optimistic Pete Harman again welcomed the new ownership. "I tried Pepsi the other day," he told a Salt Lake City reporter shortly after the transaction had been made public, "and it tasted real good."

Neither Heublein nor Reynolds "ever did a nickel's worth of retail," Harman added. "They didn't understand the business. They didn't understand how to motivate employees."

But he had high expectations for KFC's new boss, PepsiCo. "It's a breath of fresh air for KFC," Harman noted.

Other franchisees had similar opinions about the new parent company. "In keeping with Jordan's declaration that PepsiCo's success was tied, to a great degree, to new product development, Harman's was willing to be a test market for any product that PepsiCo agreed to—and many times we were testing products of our own choice," Harman said. "For example, in light of non-fried chicken competition, we tested a baked chicken recipe.

"A lot was happening at the same time. Collins Foods, which had a bunch of stores, test marketed oven-roasted chicken, while other franchisees tested build-your-own salad bars and a home-delivery system based on Pizza Hut's pretty successful model. I think a non-fried product is very important for KFC," Jordan told *Restaurants & Institutions* in November 1986. "Whether the rotisserie-cooked product KFC is testing will be the one, the consumer will tell us."

The first product to receive widespread release under the new regime were the Chicken Littles Sandwiches, which were accompanied by a national advertising campaign.

Earlier in 1986, KFC had dedicated its new $23-million, two-million-square-foot Colonel Sanders Technical Center near The Whitehouse in Louisville. Under PepsiCo, the focus at the Technical Center soon switched primarily to new product testing and training. The radial-shaped five-story building atop the hill was a technological marvel and included such then-radical features as remote control units that allowed instructors to control lights, audio-visual equipment, and slide and film projectors.

The complex of training, information, engineering, and program-development centers, along with two complete KFC restaurants, was connected to The Whitehouse via an underground tunnel. Additionally, four different kitchens were housed in the building, the largest able to hold twenty open fryers, several pressure fryers, and other equipment. Various labs were designed solely to test both new equipment and new products. The Colonel's "mug," of course, permeated the bright and airy building.

Perhaps the most telling symbolic gesture was to seal eleven sealed test tubes containing the Colonel's secret spices in the building's cornerstone.

"For all the good feelings with PepsiCo coming in, I was a little worried about all of the new products," Harman admitted later. "Although I agreed that consumers probably wanted a non-fried option, I didn't ever want to make the mistake again of getting away from our core strengths. I think Dick Mayer was having the same second thoughts. I think he was under a lot of pressure to roll out more new products faster. After all, I'm sure the folks at PepsiCo thought, 'It worked for Taco Bell—why shouldn't it work for KFC?'"

Harman's thoughts were echoed in a December 15, 1986 article in *Nation's Restaurant News*, which mused, "There remains a question whether PepsiCo, an aggressive marketer of new products, will grow impatient with KFC's cautious approach to new product growth."

But for PepsiCo Chairman and CEO D. Wayne Calloway, these were minor quibbles. He had every right to be optimistic. Despite heavy competition, KFC's market share increased through the end of 1986 to 45.3 percent of the chicken segment of the total market.

And, for the moment, that appeared to be enough.

10

A New Day

It's all about the food, of course. From China to California, from Louisville to London, it all comes back to the food. The 1980s and 1990s presented a different set of challenges for KFC. From the heady experiences of the first restaurant in Beijing to the black days of warfare between franchisees and the corporate office, KFC continued to flourish whenever this humble fact was cherished and embraced:

Have a point of difference—and drive it.

The initial point of difference, of course, is the food.

But in the increasingly overcrowed quick-service restaurant market, where new chicken restaurants popped up in th U.S. like mushrooms after a summer rain, that point of difference had to encompass even more than food. For KFC to continue strong, *everyone*, from the CEO to every restaurant general manager, had to understand that it was the *total* package—advertising, promotions, unit design and layout, cleanliness, courtesy, and quality—that was needed to separate KFC from the pack.

Internationally, KFC kept its sights set on opening new restaurants and overcoming challenges to do so.

China experts told Ta-Tung (Tony) Wang, vice president of KFC's Southeast Asia region, that the huge Chinese market was impenetrable, that the labyrinthine Beijing bureaucracy was unfathomable, and that the government would be neutral at best and hostile at worst to any American quick-service restaurant. But in early 1987, Wang told Dick Mayer that the time had come to try anyway. Mayer, who had long supported strong, sustained growth in Asia, especially by KFC-owned stores, was receptive.

> *"The Colonel represents the free enterprise system better than any individual in the world. Mao's tomb represents communism. The really great thing that happened was bringing these two opposite cultures together toward one goal."*
>
> —Pete Harman

Wang's research pointed to Beijing as the logical location for opening the first Kentucky Fried Chicken store in China. It had the most western hotels, and a significant portion of the population was relatively well-off and educated. Slowly, laboriously, Wang sifted his way through the layers of bureaucracy in his quest to establish KFC in China, advancing from:

1. The Ministry of Light Industry, to
2. The Beijing Corporation of Animal Production, to
3. The Beijing Tourist Bureau, to
4. The Foreign Economic Development Commission, to
5. The City Planning Commission

Fortunately, the recent sale of KFC to PepsiCo only strengthened Wang's hand, because PepsiCo had excellent contacts with Communist officials. With the explicit support of PepsiCo CEO Wayne Calloway, who announced PepsiCo's plan to invest $100 million in China by the mid-1990s, and a mandate from Mayer, Wang inched forward.

According to records in the KFC archives, he laboriously forged relationships with the district government in Beijing, the Commerce Department, the Taxation Department, the Health

Department, and the powerful Food, Supply, and Logistics Department. Acquiring the requisite signatures took months.

To make matters even more difficult, Wang said later that virtually *every* building in Beijing was occupied. The city also strongly enforced an arcane law that required any new tenants to hire all of the old employees from any previous establishment on the premises. Occupation of Wang's preferred location, a three-story building off Tiananmen Square, also would require the mayor's personal release and support.

Still, Wang and his general manager, Sim Kay Soon, persevered. A license to operate in Beijing finally was issued in February 1987, but, as Wang said in the years that followed, obtaining the essential water, electricity, gas, heating, and import licenses was by no means guaranteed. Even top Chinese businesses sometimes waited years for the appropriate licenses.

As the various permission forms trickled in, Wang and Soon were forced to assemble a staff that met KFC's stringent standards in a society where western-style service was virtually unknown. Still, the relatively high salaries KFC was offering meant that they had a large, talented, English-speaking labor pool to draw from.

Against all odds, Wang and his handpicked team finally succeeded. On November 12, 1987, a new million-dollar, five-hundred-seat restaurant sat at China's busiest intersection, across Tiananmen Square from the Mao Tse-tung mausoleum—China's most popular tourist attraction, with 150,000 visitors daily.

On that uncommonly bright and breezy day, the ribbon was cut for the first western-style fast-food restaurant in Beijing. The elaborate ceremony was televised live, and forty-five international reporters joined Beijing Mayor Chen Xi-Tung; American Ambassador Winston Lord; KFC Chairman and CEO Richard Mayer; Chairman Xia Jue of Beijing Kentucky Co., Ltd.; Steven V. Fellingham, president of Kentucky Fried Chicken International; Gregg Reynolds, vice-president of Public Affairs; and franchisees representing KFC's worldwide system.

Representing the 767 U.S. franchisees was Pete Harman. As the link to KFC's past and the Colonel himself, Harman was besieged by requests from news organizations from around the world, most of which had live feeds from the ceremony. For the modest man from Granger, Utah, it was a spectacle beyond his dreams as firecrackers roared, lion dancers danced, and the endless pageantry of China unfolded before the lucky few in attendance.

> *"It was the most exciting thing I've ever done. This was without a doubt the largest public relations campaign that's ever been pulled off in the entire restaurant industry."*
> —Pete Harman

After the opening banquet, Pete visited the 150-person crew at the new store. Harman was introduced as the living embodiment of the Colonel, and he was greeted with something akin to awe, according to Alan Frank, who accompanied Pete to China. Harman then spoke at length to the assembled crew, expounding on "the Harman Culture" and his own ideas for success. At one point, he personally demonstrated how to eat fried chicken with your fingers rather than with the more standard chopsticks.

"You have the prettiest chicken store in the world, and it's so nice and clean," he told them through an interpreter. "The customers are going to demand it be clean. The products are excellent, but as important as any of these factors is the fact that the customer needs friendly service. When you take the order, he has to receive a smile. And when you take his money and thank him, he has to receive another smile."

Through his interpreter, Harman made the assembled crew practice smiling three times. Harman quickly shook hands with each employee and distributed a customized pin created just for the occasion. Accompanying the pin was a personalized, signed note that read, "Best wishes for success from Colonel Sanders' very first franchisee to China's first Kentucky Fried Chicken franchise. Pete Harman, 1987."

//////

A Difficult Opening Day

The pins, of course, had been Harman's idea. But the next morning, on KFC-Beijing's first official day of business, all was not well.

"I'll tell you, we needed a Richard Sayer and a Jackie Trujillo and a Dale Hamilton in that kitchen," Pete said later, "because all Saturday they had gridlock in the lobby. The lobby held about one hundred customers standing up. It was ten cash registers long, very spacious. They had seventeen people working behind the counter, *and they had everything but chicken to serve*. The trays were all empty.

"At 1:00 PM, they closed the doors so they could wait on the hundred or so customers jamming the lobby. But the problem was they weren't cooking any chicken. Two of the cookers had broken down when I went in there, and every 'Henny Penny' cooker lid was up. There should have been something in those Henny Pennys. Pretty easy to figure out. They were reading the manual, mopping up the floor because it said to mop the floor at a certain time of the day. I had to walk out.

"They took in $7,800 that day, but one of our stores in Provo, Utah, takes in 40 to 50 percent more than that on the Fourth of July. They needed one of our district or division managers. A bunch of chicken would have been flyin' out of there."

Still, Harman found one bright spot that chaotic first morning. "When I went into the store, every one of them had their pin in the same place. Every one of those employees turned and smiled at me as I walked by. Every one, without exception.

"Then I told them, 'When the Colonel showed us how to cook the chicken, there were a few very loyal people who made that baby work in Salt Lake City, Utah, and you have the same responsibilities here right now." Afterward, Harman said he walked around the gleaming, three-story building, carefully memorizing every detail.

"When you pull up in front of the world's largest Kentucky Fried Chicken, it is very impressive," he said. "Two life-sized statues of the Colonel stand on either side of the front doors. You wonder, what's going on? It all started with just a pot of chicken on 39th South in Salt Lake City. It's a long way from 39th South to Beijing, China. Six thousand miles, to be exact."

Despite the fact that even a modest meal costs as much as a quarter of the average worker's weekly wage, Harman said the restaurant was packed from the first day. Afterward, he visited the Great Wall of China, the pandas at the Beijing Zoo, and Mao's Tomb before rejoining the official KFC party for a final banquet in Beijing. Mayor Xi-Tung delivered a formal speech, followed by short addresses from several other dignitaries, including Harman.

Pete said he was startled when the mayor followed the exchange of gifts with another, more personal speech.

"Then he walked down and threw his arms around me," Harman recalled, "and gave me a big ol' bear hug. There was a lot to that bear hug. I couldn't speak the language, but I damn well felt it. After all the pictures and tours are over, the thing I'll always remember is that neat, neat relationship. Both sides were raised just the opposite, but we were all trying to do something together and make it work.

Later, as the KFC officials debriefed following the trip, Gregg Reynolds, KFC's vice president of public affairs, said that the Chinese were most taken by Pete Harman. "How could anyone get all those employees to smile? Only Pete could have done that. No one could have represented the United States better than Pete did."

As early as 1992, the first Beijing KFC was serving 2 million customers a year, 40,000 each week, and had already been expanded to hold more than seven hundred customers. Three more KFCs soon opened in Beijing, along with two more in Shanghai.

Trouble at Home

But for all of the high spirits generated by KFC's successful launch in China, Harman said that there was a piece of unfinished business that left him uneasy. The ten-year contract that the corporation had offered franchisees in 1976 had expired, and KFC didn't seem to be in any hurry to renew it or to present a new one. Mayer had several preliminary meetings with franchisees, but nothing had been offered.

In July 1989, CEO and chairman Richard Mayer resigned and was replaced as KFC CEO by John M. Cranor, an executive who had joined PepsiCo twelve years earlier.

"It was my sense that Dick had done a pretty good job," Mike Miles said in retrospect. "He was reasonably well liked by the franchisees. What happened to Dick was that the CEO of PepsiCo, D. Wayne Calloway, didn't 'get' franchisees. Wayne was a brilliant guy, but he was a financial guy—and just didn't 'get' franchisees at all. So it was hard for Dick to work for Wayne on the one hand and be friends and supportive of the franchisees on the other hand. Without the burden of Pepsi to deal with, I think Dick would have been a very popular CEO of KFC, but he had this difficult situation to work with."

In the end, the pressure to roll out new products on a regular basis became too much, and Mayer returned to General Foods USA, where he had begun in sales and product management nearly thirty years earlier. Mayer is still highly regarded by most franchisees today.

On August 1, 1989, a copy of PepsiCo/KFC's new contract was presented to all franchisees. According to Kohl, the negative response was staggering. "When they dropped the big bomb and changed our contract, that's when the honeymoon was over and divorce court was looming."

Jackie Trujillo, then the vice-chairman at Harman Management, said that PepsiCo proposed to radically revise the franchisee renewal policy. "PepsiCo had been a good parent company," she said. "We worked fine together until it came to renewing the contract. Some of the officers at PepsiCo wanted to change our contract into a more generic one, much like the ones they already had with Taco Bell and Pizza Hut.

"Well, the current contract had been in force for a long, long time, and we're a very highly franchised company. There were a lot more franchisee stores than there were company stores. I think they had an idea that they wanted to buy everybody out anyway."

PepsiCo's new contract eliminated renewal rights, which guaranteed operators the right to sell the business to the person of their choosing. It also severely limited or eliminated the ten-year extension, mileage minimums between stores, and changed the franchisee fee. In short, it stripped the franchisees of most of their business protection.

"We tried to negotiate," Trujillo said. "Pete even went to see Calloway. He made a trip just to say, 'Is there anything you can do for us?' Of course, Calloway wouldn't get involved. He was a very nice man, but he kind of let everybody do their own thing. He didn't leave us much choice."

Spearheading the franchise owners were hard-nosed, legally astute John R. Neal, who had negotiated the original contract, and a franchisee with stores in New York, Darlene Pfeiffer. Pfeiffer had opened her first restaurant in 1966 and eventually added several more. In short order, she worked on the National Franchisee Advisory Council, the National Ad Cooperative, and became president of the Association of Kentucky Fried Chicken Franchisees (AKFCF) in 1986.

"John Cranor walked into a meeting," Pfeiffer recalled, "and he was not as nice or charismatic as Mike Miles or Dick Mayer. He threw the new contract down on the table and said, 'You will take this and accept what you have here, or you're going to have to deal with me.' He wore these big horn-rimmed glasses, and he was very, very stern. Then he said, 'You won't want to deal with me.'

"So we went into conference and immediately decided *he* was going to have to deal with *us*." The AKFCF called a franchisee-only meeting in Louisville for later in August. When the time came, hundreds of franchisees arrived from across the U.S.

According to Pete Harman, the franchisees first heard from Andrew C. Selden, the AKFCF's attorney. Selden drafted a six-point plan of action to counteract the new contract. The first point was to raise enough money to fight the contract in court.

> *"There had been a thunderstorm brewing and, at that moment, a bolt of lightning split the sky and the thunder clapped. It was like God was saying, 'Go for it. Go for it!' We all applauded—and we went for it."*
>
> —Darlene Pfeiffer

Selden's proposal called for each franchisee to donate $1,000 per store for the first year's legal expenses. As always, everyone immediately looked to Pete Harman for their next cue.

"Pete's got a heart as big as a city block," John R. Neal recalled. "He's always been there for the franchisees. When the lawsuit was being discussed in August of '89, Pete was the first one to stand up in that closed meeting and say, 'I'm here to support the $1,000-a-store levy.' Pete at that time had 250 stores, so that was a pretty big number no matter which way you cut it. We raised about $3.6 million that day. That was our war chest for year one. As seven years went by, we had to go back to the well a number of times.

"Pete also did another thing that was extremely brave for him to do. He became a plaintiff in the lawsuit. To become a plaintiff in the lawsuit, our attorneys had to screen twenty-five to thirty volunteers as to a cause of action for all the allegations for this breach of contract. Pete had contractual rights that were severely challenged by the change in this contract. He had true 'franchisee skin' in this game. He became one of the eleven plaintiffs whom we selected from a large list of franchisees who volunteered.

"Because of the lawsuit, John Cranor, who was the head of KFC worldwide, and Kyle Craig, who was the CEO of KFC-US, deemed that any plaintiff in a lawsuit against the corporation was a franchisee *not in good standing*. Such a franchisee could not build a new store or even buy a fellow franchisee's store. Pete, myself, and nine other franchisees were included.

"As this went around, I defended myself by saying, 'We are in a very elite class, because Pete Harman is at the head of the list.' There were some franchisees who had one store. It's very easy to bully them around. But Pete has always looked at the big picture."

As the lawsuit dragged on, KFC enforced the no-buy/no-build provision for the so-called persona non grata stores.

"They wouldn't let you expand," Harman recalled. "They said nobody could build a new store as long as this lawsuit was going on. I think there were five thousand stores in the United States when the lawsuit started, and when it was over, there were five thousand stores. Not one store was built. It was dumb.

"My people wanted to fight them. They really wanted to go after them."

Harman's Response

"I said, 'No, we're not going to go after anybody. Instead, we're going to make our 250 stores the best 250 stores in America. I want them better than good—I want them to be so good that KFC will have to take notice.' And that's what we did for the entire time. We concentrated solely on what we already had and poured our energy into making what we had better."

—Pete Harman

And so began the darkest years in the history of Kentucky Fried Chicken. Franchisee and franchisor worked uneasily together, and the division grew deeper each year. The AKFCF brought in Edgar Zingman of Wyatt, Tarrant & Combs to work with Selden. A few franchisees accepted Cranor's terms and were allowed to expand, but most stuck together in opposition to the 1989 contract.

"I was on committees with KFC then," Trujillo said, "and I would tell them, 'You know, you are just so stupid for thinking you are going to do this. What are you thinking? Don't you want this company to grow?' They would listen, then they would go do what they wanted to do anyway. Nothing much happened. They kept meeting with us to try to get us to negotiate, to get *us* to change, but they just wouldn't do anything."

Things weren't much better on the company side. One of the few KFC corporate employees who worked well with franchisees was Chuck Rawley. A former franchisee himself with a different concept, Rawley joined KFC in 1985 and worked his way through the corporation, beginning with a stint in a restaurant and a session in "chicken school." From there he worked as an area coach, then was brought back to Louisville to handle operations for the Chicken Littles rollout. Eventually, he rose from what was then called a district manager to VP of operations on the West Coast, vice-president for operations of the Southwest Division, then vice president of operations for KFC West. As VPO West, he was thrust into the middle of the litigation.

"Absolutely in the middle of it," Rawley said. "What we all focused on in the field was making sure that we ran great restaurants. We didn't get into it. That was not our fight. It was not our obligation to try to resolve it.

"There was a lot of mistrust during that time," Rawley said, "but I believe that those of us who were on the operations side, who reached out to the franchisees and worked with them as if nothing were going on, got credit for progress. We were much more in tune with the day-to-day business, as opposed to over-arching contractual disputes."

Neal said it wasn't long before KFC realized they weren't helping the brand by alienating their first, their largest, and their most powerful franchisee, Pete Harman. "That was a very tough position to be in because all the other ten of us hid behind Pete," Neal said. "If Pete is persona non grata, so are we. Pete couldn't build stores, or buy stores, or do great things for the brand.

"Finally, one day at a convention old John Cranor had to stand up and eat crow. He said, 'Well, we've rethought this franchisee-not-in-good-standing rule. And since the lawsuit was filed years before we adopted this policy, then that exempts Pete and the other ten plaintiffs in the case. But from this day forward, anybody that sues will be a franchisee not in good standing."

> *"The Colonel and his two daughters loved franchisees—just loved them. He loved people so much that they became a part of his family. Consequently, when I became a franchisee, I became a part of a culture. Not a franchise organization, not a company—a family. To this day, we have that family feeling."*
>
> —Darlene Pfeiffer

A Ray of Optimism

As always, Harman Management Corporation forged quietly ahead. Even during KFC's stormiest days, Pete remained focused on making his stores better and empowering his employees.

In time, his approach drew national attention:

> *"Most executives assume that as their organization grows, they have to sacrifice the closeness to employees that is possible in a smaller business—if they attempted it in the first place. Pete Harman, the first and largest Kentucky Fried Chicken franchisee, argues otherwise. His people-oriented style is reflected through his five-thousand-member organization. The result is a unique, cohesive, and wildly successful company."*
>
> —Tom Peters, in *On Achieving Excellence*

"Most companies lose their best people," Harman told the editors. "We don't. We give them a chance to grow with us."

As he had done since the Do Drop Inn days, Harman accomplished this by lavishing his top performers with ownership, incentives, praise, acknowledgement, and regular communication. Consequently, Harman Management enjoyed an 85-percent retention of managers and about 20 percent higher volume per store than the average KFC outlet in the late 1980s.

On Achieving Excellence also reported how Harman recognized management trainees, 80 percent of whom started with the company.

Motivating Managers

▶ An annual seven-day manager's retreat in a resort setting with the focus on team-building within the organization.

▶ Six meetings a year with Harman, who visits all restaurants an average of twice a year.

▶ Milestone awards for managers who achieve million-dollar sales, 1.5 million and two million and above, high percentage volume increases, or longevity awards.

▶ A Top Ten Award presented to restaurant general managers/owners, and their co-managers/owners, and to area consultants and regional directors who are the top 10 percent of performers by volume, profitability, and service.

▶ Awards are presented at the end of every fiscal year in a formal banquet for the top 25 percent of managers and their spouses.

▶ The number-one rated manager each year wins a free trip for two to anywhere in the world—or $8,000.

In October 1990, the prestigious *Restaurant Business* magazine named Harman Management Corp. its "1990 Company of the Year." In dedicating the award, the magazine's editors had this to say:

> *"This industry pioneer in human resources—innovator in employee motivation and customer satisfaction—proves that growth opportunities still exist for wise professionals in our industry. With a sound family ethic-and-reward system, the company—Kentucky Fried Chicken's first and now largest domestic franchisee—has long enjoyed high profits and incredibly low turnover. The RB Company of the Year Award caps off a big year of industry recognition for Harman Management: Jackie Trujillo, executive vice chairman and founding member of The Women's Forum, is a 1990 RB Leadership Award winner. Meanwhile, Leon 'Pete' Harman*

won the coveted IFMA (International Foodservice Manu-
facturers Association) Gold Plate Award as the 1990 food-
service operator of the year.

"From Louisville to Beijing, and in knowledgeable cir-
cles throughout the food service industry, the name Harman
Management Corp. is synonymous with people-oriented
management, customer satisfaction, fast-food innovation,
and industry leadership."

RB's rapturous article pointed out that while forty-five of its
stores have reached $1 million or more, Harman Management
spends the equivalent of more than 1.5 percent of its annual
sales of $178 million on people-oriented management practices.
"We never brag about how much money we make," Harman
told *RB*. "But we're very big about celebrating the successes of
our people."

Harman's Keys to Success

▶ Ownership
▶ Encouragement
▶ Recognition
▶ Empowerment

At one point in the interview, Pete mentioned that his
future father-in-law had once dismissively called him a
"hasher"—slang for a cook in a greasy roadside restaurant
with little talent and no future.

"I never believed we were hashers," Pete said.

"Eat Where It All Began"

For one bright moment in the fall of 1990, franchisees and
franchisors put aside their differences and celebrated the Colonel's one-hundredth birthday. On September 9, hundreds of
them traveled to Corbin, Kentucky, where John R. Neal had

overseen the restoration of the Colonel's Harland Sanders Café—where it all began. Neal and a team of restoration specialists in historic preservation had spent two years meticulously restoring the restaurant to its original state. Almost miraculously, the original ceiling, wall, and floor materials from the 1940s were uncovered and quickly conserved. A museum honoring both the Colonel and his creation was also installed.

The first visitor was the Colonel's widow, Claudia Sanders. The first piece of chicken cooked in the faithfully restored restaurant—using the Colonel's original recipe of eleven herbs and spices, of course—was presented to Pete Harman.

"Colonel Sanders was a true visionary, a pioneer in what has become a global quick-service restaurant industry," Cranor said. "His commitment to customer service is legendary. And he foresaw a growing consumer demand for convenience that has never abated."

Colonel Quotes

You have to be optimistic. I've heard people complain about the weather. There's no such thing as bad weather, just different kinds of good weather.

Perfection is just barely good enough.

If you're a dreamer, then do it—back up your dreams. A dream is just a suggestion to you to start something out, to do something.

Service is the best thing in the world you can give.

I believe a man'll rust out quicker than he'll wear out. (On his often-stated desire to work until he was a hundred years old.)

I took care of orphans and God took care of me. He does it every time. (On good deeds and good fortune.)

But any good feelings between franchisees and KFC leadership dissipated when the corporate office purchased 209 franchises from Collins Foods International's U.S. division. That was followed by the purchase of 182 franchise stores in Canada. By the end of 1990, KFC owned 32 percent of the total American operating units, as compared with the franchisees' 68 percent.

The strain was having an impact in other areas, including PepsiCo's much-publicized new products. Other chains had vaulted ahead of Kentucky Fried Chicken with their chicken nuggets.

A New Name, a Change of Pace

In 1991, the corporation codified what had been common practice for years—officially changing the name of Kentucky Fried Chicken to "KFC" on all signage and advertising. The new "Speedmark" logo also signaled an end to the old "down-home" personality and paved the way for KFC's entry into non-fried chicken.

Fortunately, the classic red and white stripes were retained, as was the Colonel's beaming "mug."

According to business writer Frances E. Norton, by 1991 KFC admitted that constantly introducing new products hadn't worked.

"Once again, the corporate boys figured out that a back-to-basics approach worked best," Harman said. "They postponed their new menus. They caught up to the rest of the country with a new $20-million computer system that did everything from control fryer cooking times to linking the manager's office and drive-through window back to company headquarters.

"I think that by the end of 1991, for the first time pre-tax profits for overseas operations passed profits for the U.S. market. Since they'd effectively shut down growth in the U.S., PepsiCo had pumped money into new stores abroad." Not surprisingly, by the end of 1992, sales and profits from the international units doubled. Harman said that announcement signaled the beginning of an overseas building boom. KFC built an average of one non-U.S. unit per day during the early 1990s.

"They tried out a whole bunch of stuff overseas during this period," Harman said. "Delivery, supermarket kiosks, mall and office-building snack shops, mobile trailer units, satellite units, kiosks in stadiums and airports—you name it, they tried it.

"Some ideas worked pretty well, particularly along the Pacific Rim. Those they brought to the U.S. But some concepts bled off business from established stores. Cranor really poured a lot of KFC resources overseas. About the only thing new that worked at all in the states was the 'limited time only' (LTO) concept."

"We'd try the LTOs for a few weeks and really pump up the advertising," Harman added. "That always seemed to give the stock a nice boost on Wall Street."

But what concerned Pete and other franchisees the most was how KFC was systematically buying up their fellow franchisees. Following the blockbuster purchase of Jim Collin's mammoth West Coast operation, in 1991

> **Popular KFC LTOs**
>
> *Hot 'n' Spicy Chicken*
> *Honey BBQ Wings*
> *Skinfree Crispy*
> *Oriental Wings*
> *Hot Shots*
> *Popcorn Chicken*

PepsiCo underwrote the purchase of Scott's restaurants, as well as Solomon's (twenty-three stores on Long Island), McFarland's (twenty-eight stores in Indianapolis), and Ash's (thirty stores in Jacksonville, Florida). In 1992, KFC also bought out Cornett (thirty-six stores in the Northeast), Fitzpatrick (fifty-two stores, mostly in the north central U.S.), and White (seventy-two stores, all in the Northeast).

"But the rest of us held together," Harman said. "We knew the best way for Kentucky Fried Chicken to grow was to have a strong base of stores owned by individuals who cared about what the Colonel had tried to do, who remained faithful to the Colonel's vision."

Harman liked Wayne Calloway personally, but never thought PepsiCo understood the chicken business. What worked in sodas didn't necessarily work in a consumer-driven product where people sat down and ate a certain kind of chicken.

"I know there were people working hard in Louisville," he said. "I know there were people in Louisville who cared about this product. Neither side thought it could afford to give an inch. Somebody was going to have to step forward and make this thing work."

That somebody was David C. Novak.

David Novak Steps In

David Novak was handpicked by Calloway to replace Cranor. Novak had held leadership positions at PepsiCo for twenty years in marketing and operations before coming to KFC. He inherited a company split by a war between franchisee and franchisor, losing ground to other brands, and underperforming both in the individual stores and on Wall Street.

He could hardly wait to get started.

> *"When I came to KFC, I walked into an environment where people weren't really working together, first and foremost. We had a great brand—90 percent of America ate the product at least once a year. It was highly recognizable."*
> —David Novak

"PepsiCo had acquired KFC nine years earlier, and for nine years KFC had never achieved its business goals in PepsiCo, so we were their ugly duckling. When I got this job, most people thought I was being sent to an unfixable situation. Over the previous six years, same-store sales growth had been flat to negative. We had a lawsuit going on, and I found that the franchisees hated the company. 'Hate' is a strong word, but it comes as close to that as you could get. And the company hated the franchisees. Nobody trusted each other.

"The company people blamed the franchisees for where we were because the franchisees controlled the marketing process.

They had more votes, so we couldn't hire and fire the advertising agency. So the advertising agency was viewed to be in the franchisees' hip pocket. We couldn't get the kind of quality we really needed from them. We couldn't get the products in because the franchisees wouldn't do this, wouldn't do that."

When Novak arrived, it had been years since franchisees had even been invited to Louisville.

"It was sort of like a franchisee was something we had to deal with, versus somebody we had to work with," he said. "And the company person from the franchise perspective was someone who had a separate agenda that was different than his. Neither side had a true appreciation of what each of them could bring to the party."

"From my experience working with Pizza Hut franchisees and Pepsi-Cola Bottlers," Novak recalled. "I discovered that they offer a great wealth of talent. If you look at them that way, they can give you an expertise and experience level that you need when you come into any business.

> *"I think probably the biggest thing that I did, coming into the situation, was realizing that the formula we had applied wasn't working. Things had to be different."*
>
> —David Novak

"Franchisees give you an honest perspective, because they are in their stores, they listen to customers, and they tell it like it is. They don't have any political agenda, or corporate agenda, or whatever. All they want to do is grow their business, drive profits, and make sure that their family moves ahead, and the people they work with move ahead. At least the good ones are that way.

"We had to change the game."

Within a few days of Novak's arrival in Louisville, a meeting of the opposing sides was scheduled. Several people within the organization approached him privately and said, "We want you to cancel it. We don't think you ought to talk to them because you're not ready to talk to them. You don't know the business well enough."

Novak's response was swift and characteristic:

"I said, 'Look, I'm going to talk to the franchisees. I'm going to tell them how we're going to work together, how we're going to have to go through a process, but we're going to work together as partners as we move forward.'"

By all accounts, the meeting was a success. Novak laid out his plan to learn the business by visiting the franchisees. But he made no elaborate promises, nor did he comment on the pending litigation.

"I told everybody at corporate that I loved franchisees. I said, 'I don't want to hear a bad thing about franchisees ever again. The franchisees are our partners. And yeah, we're going to have issues. We're going to argue about things. We're going to have debates. But I want you to *like* franchisees. We're going to have a different attitude around here.'"

Transformation

According to franchisee and corporate executives alike, that initial meeting set off a chain reaction that would transform KFC. True to his word, Novak went on a mission to understand the franchisees. He appeared at every regional association and grilled franchisees on their livelihood.

By now, Chuck Rawley had been promoted to chief operations officer for KFC and had been charged with coordinating the KFC/Taco Bell two-in-one program and new home-delivery systems throughout the KFC system as well.

Since arriving in 1985, Rawley had seen six KFC presidents come and go.

"David brought something that the others didn't," he said. "Prior to David, it was very much of a desk-jockey type job. Very much marketing oriented. The previous presidents really didn't understand the restaurant business, didn't understand the issues and the complexities, thought of it more in a packaged-goods kind of environment.

"It's not a packaged-goods business, it's very retail oriented, it's very point-of-consumer-contact oriented, it's very much consumer focused. Everything about food in general is critical. The most important thing is the 'people' side of things."

According to Rawley, that was the part of the equation that was very much missing within the organization.

"Not that the people were bad," he said, "it was the lack of leadership and motivation. Trust in their own capabilities wasn't there. I was a member of that team and felt that in myself. We were self-doubting: 'Are we really able to make this happen?'

"David started with the franchisees, going out visiting, understanding the business, the issues, and then starting the cultural revolution within KFC."

Novak's Three Questions

➤ "What is working?"
➤ "What is not working?"
➤ "What would you do if you were in my position?"

"I learned a lot in the whole process," Novak said in describing his visits with franchisees. "You had to be humble because people were very upset with past leadership. I was part of PepsiCo, part of a group of people that I know were working hard. A lot of people said, 'You better be good, son.' Sometimes it was kind of insulting, but I just said, 'Well, I hope I'm good, too.' I turned the other cheek and listened—really listened—and tried to understand. I let them get it off their chests."

Novak then repeated the process with KFC's corporate employees. "I got people working together around the common goal of fixing the business," he said. "Everybody wanted me to solve the contract. I told people at the beginning, 'I'm not going to solve the contract until we fix the business. Once we get the business going, *then* I'll think about solving the contract. Our big priority is to fix the business."

One of Novak's first stops, like John Y. Brown and Mike Miles before him, was to visit Los Altos and meet with Pete Harman and Jackie Trujillo.

"The Harman organization was the role-model organization from what I had seen," Novak said. "When I first spoke to the KFC franchisees, Jackie Trujillo was also there. She talked about how important it is to work with your people. It really touched me, I thought it was great. I couldn't wait to get out there and be with the Harman organization.

"The first time was right after I joined KFC. Before I went to casual wear, I sat there with a tie on. As I was meeting with Pete, learning about his organization, I was immediately very impressed. Suddenly, Pete gets up, goes into his office and comes back with his 'Harman pin.'

"He said, 'You know what? 'You're going to be the best thing that ever happened to KFC. I believe in you. You're going to be the greatest leader that we've had in a long time— and boy, do we need you.' He took my very expensive tie and pinned his Harman pin on it. Then he said, 'I give this to recognize people.'

"He ruined my favorite tie, but at the same time he also made me feel good. He believes in spontaneous recognition. He's been doing that for a long time, so we were philosophically aligned. In terms of what I wanted to do, he was already doing it. It gave me more courage of my conviction that I was going in the right direction."

Novak created "Promise Pride," a program that recognized and celebrated the top 10 percent of KFC's company operators. He also invited franchisees to participate in the program.

"I basically ripped off Pete's program because it made a lot of sense," Novak said. "I looked for ways to dramatically recognize people, and he just spurred me on because of his philosophy."

When Novak announced the Promise Pride incentive in '95, Trujillo set a goal for Harman Management to be the first franchise in the system to make 100 percent Promise Pride.

"We wanted all of our stores—and we had 265 at the time—all to be Promise Pride certified and be the best in the system," Jim Olson recalled.

That ambitious tenacity for excellence and food quality, Trujillo said, is a direct inheritance from Pete Harman.

"It's still all about the food," she said. "All of the wonderful new programs, the multibranding, the overseas expansion, the renewed emphasis today on freshness—it still comes back to the food. We better have a product that people want. David Novak understands that kind of commitment. It has been a part of Pete's culture since the Do Drop Inn days.

"That's Pete's attitude. He is out to please his customers. And he does whatever it takes."

> *"I love how when Pete goes into a store, he goes over and puts his arm around everybody and thanks them. I do the same things."*
> —David Novak

Novak brought in Senn-Delaney, a California-based "culture company," to help establish just such a recognition-based system within the KFC system.

"David's objective was to bring the company and the franchisees together to understand each other's issues and concerns," Rawley said, "and to really bond with a KFC family, as opposed to a company and a franchise family. It was a cultural revolution.

"Until then, there was no excitement, there was no motivation, no recognition—it didn't even feel like a restaurant company. I think David sensed that immediately and began to really reinvent a culture that was recognition oriented. People first, having fun, really building our core operating values that are posted all over the building today."

One of Novak's first changes was largely symbolic—but highly evocative. He changed the name of the Louisville office complex from "KFC World Headquarters" to "Restaurant Support Center."

"It says something to the people working in the building, that we're here to support our number-one leader, which is our restaurant general manager," Rawley said. "That store-level execution is what this business is all about, and we need to be here for one reason, to support our number-one leaders, whatever it takes. Operations are the key, and the key to that is to have the right restaurant managers. You show me a good restaurant manager and I'll show you a good restaurant."

With a Good Manager—

▶ You don't have "Help Wanted'" signs hanging in the windows.

▶ You don't have the turnover at 200-plus percent.

▶ You don't have the operational issues.

▶ You don't have cleanliness issues.

▶ You do have a good, well-run restaurant.

Novak melded the Harman model, the results of his face-to-face meetings with franchisees and their breakout sessions, the results of an intensive survey sent to every restaurant manager, and the concepts preached by Senn-Delaney into a cultural revolution at KFC.

"There weren't any restaurant operations involved in it," Rawley recalled. "It wasn't like, 'This is how you bread chicken.' It's 'This is how you treat people, and this is how you will be successful or how you will fail.'"

Novak's other changes were more practical.

One of the most frequent complaints from franchisees was that KFC no longer made chicken the way the Colonel used to make it. Novak gathered the original experts on Original Recipe chicken to develop a solution.

"We decided that we needed to marinate the chicken back in the store," he said. "That was the first initiative—to get our fried chicken back to the way it ought to be.

"It galvanized the organization around quality. This was the key thing we needed to do. What was really interesting was that after we went through this process, the first year the sales were a little bit better than they had been."

A second quiet revolution came when someone in marketing called Novak and told him that a group of franchisees in Texas had developed Crispy Strips and were getting 10 percent sales growth with them.

In the previous regime, this kind of entrepreneurship would have been stifled. Novak instead said, "Well gee, let's understand this. Let's get down there."

Novak said that KFC was among the last major chains to offer chicken strips, because its research-and-development department had maintained that the poultry industry couldn't supply enough quality chicken breasts to meet KFC's potential demand.

"Meanwhile, every casual dining chain in the world had crispy strips—bad ones, not the good ones we now make," Novak said. "We went down to Texas, learned about the process, and the franchisees helped us figure out how we could solve the supply issues. Our R&D people worked together, commercialized it, and made it a national idea. When we rolled it out, we had double-digit sales growth—and it added hundreds of thousands of dollars in sales *and* was instrumental in turning the business around."

Emboldened, Novak created the KFC Chef's Council with six franchisees, including Pete Harman, Tim West, George Tinsley, and Jerry Haynie, and two "chefs" from the KFC kitchens. The operators would arrive with their recipes, and they would sample new products all day. From these sessions with the Chef's Council, KFC developed several new products, including Chunky Chicken Pot Pies.

Both Harman and Tinsley had learned to cook chicken from the Colonel himself.

"Since the days when the Colonel shook hands with customers in his first restaurant in Corbin, Kentucky, one of the greatest strengths at KFC has always been its relationship with the customer," Haynie said. "This council shows that we still listen to what our customers have to say. If they don't like it, we won't make it. It's that simple."

"The key to a successful product is great taste," Harman added. "If we don't think it tastes fantastic, we go back to the drawing board and try again."

Also emerging from the Chef's Council were directions on how to offer roasted chicken in pieces as well as the instantly popular Colonel's Crispy Strips and Twister Wraps.

"I'm a big believer in creating a culture and a fun work environment, a big believer in teamwork," Novak said. "What I did was start a cultural revolution around common values. It brought us all together, it created one common culture."

Floppy Chicken Time

The walls of Novak's office are covered with photos of Novak posing with employees. And in most of the pictures, someone is holding a bright yellow rubber chicken.

"Everybody has his or her own recognition tool; I started giving away a floppy chicken," he said. "I'd go out in the market place, I'd see a cook who had been in the restaurant for thirty years, I'd say, 'Gee, thanks a lot. Here's a floppy chicken.' I write on the floppy chicken, take their picture, and tell them it's going to be in my office. Then I'd say, 'I'll send you a copy of the picture.' Then I give them a hundred dollars, because you can't eat a floppy chicken.

"I didn't want to give away a clock or a watch or a plaque, because that's boring. I wanted to have something that says we're in a fun business, we need to recognize our people—and it's a big part of what makes it work in the restaurant."

Soon other managers began giving out their version of the floppy chicken, including Chuck Rawley's bulldogs. Slowly, the franchisee's perceptions of the corporate office in Louisville began to change. And with that sea change came a distinct improvement in the bottom line.

"When someone asks me, 'How did you turn around KFC?' I always tell them, 'If you ask the finance people, they will tell you it's because we introduced the Colonel's Crispy

Strips, Pot Pie, Tender Roast Chicken in Pieces, and had the product news to turn around the business.

"But *I* tell you the reason why *we* turned around KFC is the triumph of human spirit. It's people working together—all those ideas came forward because people were working together. We created openness. Instead of fighting each other, we started to focus on satisfying the customer and beating competition. As a result, we made steady improvement that's helped us grow the business. And we doubled sales and profits over five years."

"It was totally an attitude change," Rawley said. "That alone had the biggest and longest-lasting impact. It's a feeling that you are an important person, that we value you, we value your opinion. We have certain rules and guidelines, naturally, but beyond that, we want you, our RGMs, to be the owner of that restaurant. Manage it as if you own it. We restructured bonus programs as incentive to more ownership.

"We did a lot of things right out of Harman's book. And recognition became a big part of our culture. Everybody got the little simple recognition. It's not always a trip to Florida. A lot of the time it's nothing more than a simple 'Thank you' and a pat on the back for a job well done."

As if to underline Rawley's words, in July 1996, Harman Management Corporation received yet another award for doing exactly that for forty-four years. *Nation's Restaurant News* named Harman as the winner of the 1996 Pioneer Award.

> *"Pete Harman is a master motivator and his philosophy of tying success to people, not dollars, is an industry model. During a career that has spanned half a century, he has proven that sharing ownership with employees and investing in their job satisfaction, training, and motivation are consistent with long-term success in business."*
> —James C. Doherty, Publisher, *Nation's Restaurant News*

Peace at Last

Meanwhile, the franchisee lawsuit had inched its way through the courts. LaRue Kohl said that the paperwork eventually passed through the hands of four federal judges—two of whom died and a third retired—before it finally saw resolution. In 1997, at the urging of Novak and on the heels of several successful years, PepsiCo withdrew the 1989 contract. Franchisees retained most of their hard-won rights under a new contract.

"It is probably the best contract out there," Jackie Trujillo said. "Both sides gave a little bit. We gave some and they gave some. As a result, we were all happy and ready to grow again and the system is a lot stronger now."

More importantly, the new contract signaled the beginning of a new culture at KFC.

The Future:
KFC and Pete Harman

Everything that transpired over KFC's long and storied past converged in the formation of Tricon Global Restaurants, Inc. with Taco Bell and Pizza Hut. As president and CEO of Tricon, Novak was able to take the lessons he'd learned at KFC and translate them on a corporation-wide basis. The subsequent transformation was not a revolution, but an evolution, a corporate culture that celebrated a core group of values.

From the beginning, Novak instituted a basic tenet that soon became his personal hallmark:

Recognition is a powerful way to
attract and keep good people.

Ultimately, Novak's recipe for success created something larger still, something with a proven track record for success regardless where it is applied to a single store or 30,000 stores. The secrets first identified by the Colonel and Pete Harman, coupled with

Novak's own long experience in corporate culture, provided both a continuity and foundation for the future for one of the world's most beloved brands—KFC.

The Birth of Tricon . . . and Beyond

In January 1997, PepsiCo, Inc. announced plans to spin off its restaurant division to shareholders as an independent company.

PepsiCo CEO Roger Enrico announced that the spin-off would be to everybody's benefit. "Our goal in taking these steps is to dramatically sharpen PepsiCo's focus. Our restaurant business has tremendous financial strength and a very bright future. However, given the distinctly different dynamics of restaurants and packaged goods, we believe all our businesses can better flourish with two separate and distinct managements and corporate structures."

David Novak, who had been named to head Pizza Hut as well as KFC a year before the split, had plenty to be happy about. With his leadership, PepsiCo's restaurant division had grown at the rate of 22 percent compounded over the previous five years. When the spin-off was complete, on October 7, 1997, Novak was named vice chairman and president of Tricon Global Restaurants, Inc. Andrall E. Pearson was selected to serve as chairman and CEO. And the new company chose "YUM" as its corporate symbol for the New York Stock Exchange.

Thousands of KFC, Taco Bell, and Pizza Hut employees participated in a special "Founder's Day" celebration, featuring a worldwide teleconference originating from Louisville.

"Our recipe for success starts with the belief that everything we do is about putting a YUM on people's faces," Novak said to the huge audience, "giving them the food they crave at comeback prices, combined with customer-focused teams who deliver service second to none."

From the beginning, Novak was fully aware of the problems—and the potential—in running Tricon. "We've got a lot more work to do, but the business is so much better because we are truly working together. We started this culture here at KFC, and that's why I made Louisville the corporate head-quarters for Tricon. I wanted to transform the culture we started here and do it at Taco Bell and Pizza Hut—and do it around the world. I wanted people to come into this building and feel the spirit."

Novak insisted that the first Tricon stock certificates be issued featuring portrait engravings of KFC, Pizza Hut, and Taco Bell RGMs, with the inscription, "Restaurant General Manager is No. 1."

Novak also immediately involved franchisees in operating the business by creating a franchisee advisory council, repre-senting key franchisees from all three brands.

Additionally, Jackie Trujillo was appointed to Tricon's Board of Directors.

Novak said that he was invoking the spirit of Pete Har-man's recognition culture to help shape the new company:

"That's what Pete Harman is all about. I would never pretend to be in the same league as Pete Harman, but we're kindred souls. He is a very giving person. He knows that leadership is a privilege. He knows that he's been blessed to be in a position

> *"Our formula for success: Build people capability first, then you'll satisfy the customer, then you'll make more money."*
> —David Novak

like this. I certainly feel the same way. My feeling is that I have a chance to touch 725,000 people across Tricon and make the world better through how we treat people and get results.

"My objective is to demonstrate that you can *recognize* your way to success, that our 'people first' approach gets fan-tastic results, and that people will want to emulate what we do here at Tricon. To do this, we make our people really happy employees. If they feel great about it, then we make *our* cus-tomers very happy. If we do this, then someday others will want to copy *our* formula. We can help other people do the same thing . . . and make the world a little bit better place."

One of the keys, Novak believed, was focusing on the team member of each of Tricon's restaurants around the world.

"Every great organization has that intangible difference," he said. "It's the difference between the great Green Bay Packer teams and some other team. There is an intangible culture that Green Bay had, this belief in each other that when they had to win, they could count on each other. There is a spirit behind it all, a belief that you're in the best possible place you can possibly be. That's what the great organizations have. You go to Harman's—they've got that in spades."

David Novak Takes Charge

In January 2001, Novak, then forty-eight years old, succeeded Andrall Pearson as chairman of Tricon's board of directors. Pearson, then seventy-five, continued as a company director with the title of founding chairman. With the new title, a number of observers applauded Novak's adroit orchestration of the emerging new Tricon culture into a single, successful entity.

His ascension was both expected and welcomed at Harman Management Corp.

"David is a gifted marketer," Pete Harman said. "I have no doubt he'll bring to Tricon what he brought to KFC—creativity and energy. Obviously, I think he's doing a good job because he's doing things the way we do them: with plenty of recognition, fun, and ownership. My sense is that this approach will spread easily to Taco Bell and Pizza Hut as well. He's really smart in things like advertising and new products. But where I look for him to have the greatest impact will be as the leader for all of the companies of Tricon."

Other franchisees were equally enthusiastic, including John R. Neal, who had seen every KFC leader since the Colonel himself.

Looking Ahead—An Even Bolder KFC

Novak is confident that KFC will continue to play a significant role in Tricon's future and that there is plenty of opportunity for future expansion—especially internationally:

"We actually make more profit today internationally at KFC than we do domestically. KFC is bigger than McDonald's in a lot of countries. Look at the growth potential that we have.

"We have 6,000 KFCs internationally. We could easily double that in the next five to eight years. That's where a lot of our growth is going to come from. We opened up 950 Tricon restaurants outside of the United States in 2001 on top of more than 900 in 2000. Combined with multibranding in the U.S., the international reach is what really gives us the opportunity to be a dynamic growth company."

And nowhere is that growth potential greater than in mainland China. China's more than 1.2 billion people are served by only five hundred KFCs. KFC is the number-one brand in China, according to ACNielsen's independent research.

"Not number-one *restaurant* brand, but the number-one brand in *all* of China—ahead of Nike, Coca-Cola, Disney, Pepsi, any kind of brand," Novak said. "We have a character called Chicky, who is the Ronald McDonald of China. The KFC jingle, with Chicky doing the song and dance, is in the schools in China.

"It's staggering how big we can be in China. I expect someday that we'll have more restaurants in China than we have in the United States.

"We have a tremendous operator, a tremendous general manager, in Sam Su. We have a great team, and we have people who understand the Chinese culture running the business. We built KFC China to be a powerhouse, to be better than McDonald's, and we've become better than McDonald's in China. Our food is preferred."

> *"I tell people that what we want to do is take the KFCs that we have in China, Malaysia, Hong Kong, Japan and some of our Middle Eastern countries, and bring them to the United States."*
>
> —David Novak

The man who masterminds KFC's overseas thrust, along with Pizza Hut and Taco Bell, is Pete Bassi, president, Tricon Restaurants International. While he is responsible for all of KFC's efforts internationally, clearly China is a favorite topic.

"A lot of times people ask, 'Why do you have a great business in one country and not in another?'" Bassi said. "We're really fortunate that the guy who runs KFC in China today, who got there when there were seven restaurants, did a great job of building the business, building the brand. He recognized that the people there loved the product and that there was an opportunity for a really first-class American dining experience. He developed the business even faster than McDonald's has. We're slightly bigger than McDonald's and considerably stronger there.

"We tapped the hearts and minds of the people who could afford us. We understood that only the top 2 or 3 percent were going to be able to afford us, but we did a great job of developing a brand that appealed to what they needed."

In September 2001, *The Los Angeles Times* featured what it called KFC's "Chinese blitzkrieg" in a front-page article titled "Ruling the Roost in China." Much of the lengthy article was devoted to how KFC-China had co-opted McDonald's once-invincible stranglehold on children's programs.

> *"KFC has developed a new secret recipe—measured expansion, cagey marketing, and cheerful service—and the customers are flocking in."*
>
> —*The Los Angeles Times*

"We have a stronger kids' program in China than McDonald's does," Bassi said. "We are *the* place to go for kids. The average KFC in China has four hundred kids' parties a year, more than one for every day in every restaurant. What it speaks to is the breadth of appeal that we've established with the KFC brand. I think that we're doing a terrific job of building that brand, with great facilities, great food, and the kid programs. We're standing for the same thing as a high-quality American quick-service restaurant experience—and it's given us a great foothold."

Rising Sun Smiles on KFC

Although China clearly dominates the spotlight, Bassi and others express a fondness for the KFC experience in Japan which quietly has become a cultural phenomenon. The key, according to Bassi and others, is Shin Okawara.

"We recently celebrated our thirtieth anniversary in Japan," Bassi said. "Shin Okawara, who runs the business today in Japan, was the first restaurant manager, so he's actually grown up with the system.

"I think what Japan did, probably more than any other country, is link to the Kentucky colonel culture. For years, in the seventies and early eighties, they used "My Old Kentucky Home" as the background music in their advertising. They really tried to bring in 'Southern'—especially Kentucky—culture in their branding of the business. In China, we didn't try to show pictures of the Colonel, we just tried to come across as an American mainstream brand. But in Japan, the roots of the business are much more Colonel and heritage.

"The Japanese respect for the elderly is something that America has a tough time fathoming. The Colonel just *stuck* in Japan. That's why there is a statue of the Colonel in most of the restaurants.

"Shin Okawara talks about Pete Harman all the time. And Shin has met the Colonel. These guys have linkage to the roots of KFC in the states. Japan is probably much more rooted into KFC memorabilia than any other market. When I went there for the anniversary, a couple of franchisees came up to me and said, 'Did you know the Colonel?' They won't ask me that in any other market."

> "*Fragility in food is a good thing. It means it is fresh. We serve it as soon as possible. The company says that you can hold chicken for two hours. We cut that down to forty minutes.*"
> —Shin Okawara

Japanese customers are extremely loyal to their individual stores. Through that loyalty, Okawara and his staff have been able to position KFC as a crucial part of a popular Japanese holiday.

"Every Christmas, we sell commemorative Christmas Party plates," Okawara said. "We succeeded in creating the new custom in Japan. On Christmas Eve, most families eat Kentucky Fried Chicken instead of turkey. They have to reserve a special pack—ten pieces of chicken, salad, dessert and everything—one month in advance.

"We issue a new plate with it, the Christmas plate, and people display those plates every year. On Christmas Eve, people line up for two hours to get their chicken dinner. We have a Colonel Sanders statue in every one of our stores and, during Christmas week, we put him in Santa Claus clothes. I would like to create 'Christmas in Summer,' too. That would be very difficult, but we wish we had another Christmas.

"As far as our employees are concerned, the Colonel is the most important person. He visited Japan three times before he passed away. Since then, we have followed his way of doing business. He really liked our operation.

"We have our custom and tradition to respect old, senior people, and the Colonel became part of it. Every one of the Japanese franchisees now has the Colonel's statue in bronze in every one of his or her offices."

For years, most KFC commercials in Japan concentrated on showing the beauty of Kentucky's bluegrass region. Consequently, KFC has become such a pervasive part of Japanese life that a recent study showed that more than 60 percent of Japanese respondents are reminded of Kentucky Fried Chicken and Stephen Foster's music (the "theme" music for commercials) whenever the word "Kentucky" is mentioned.

"When Japanese viewers see our commercials, they are reminded of good old America—very healthy, 'bluegrass,' and blue, clear water," Okawara said. "We are very proud of that."

"Because of our success, at one time fourteen different fast-food companies tried to copy us. As of today, we are the only one still here. They were the copiers, we had the original.

"We are really doing well. Although our product was brought from overseas, after thirty years our product has become a part of Japanese people's life, especially for Christmas and for happy occasions like birthdays or family home gatherings. That's what we are proud of."

KFC in Japan

Garden salad with cream cheese triangles

Pumpkin pudding

Earl Grey Tea pudding

Choice of vegetable or cream corn soup

Rice balls

Fried in soy sauce

Steamed with sesame and wakame (seaweed)

Curried chicken salad in pita bread

Spinach au gratin

Herb chicken (domestically produced chicken fed with a special diet of herbs and Vitamin E)

KFC's Conquest of Europe

Bassi conceded that Novak's remark about importing the KFC experience in China and Japan back to the United States and Western Europe has more than a ring of truth. He said that KFC's problem abroad is not cultural differences or differing local tastes. Instead, it originated—in many cases—with KFC itself and its early operators.

"In the U.K., KFC had a tired image for the last five years. I think that tired image lasted until we started building these freestanding restaurants with drive-throughs outside of London, and that's when things began to change."

Conversely, KFC has limited penetration in several heavily populated European countries, including France, Spain, Italy, the Netherlands, and Germany.

"We have five hundred KFCs in the U.K. that are doing fantastic," Novak said. "We only have twenty-five in Germany, twenty-five in Spain, ten in France, and five in the Netherlands. We've expanded in the U.K., so there's no reason why we can't do it in these other countries. Taking KFC into continental Europe, that's the big opportunity for us."

Bassi is convinced that the tide may be turning. A new KFC opened outside Paris in the summer of 2001 that in its first months of operation generated a higher volume than KFC International's top-performing restaurants in Beijing, Chin Zin (outside Hong Kong), and Shanghai—all of which typically earn between $3 million and $4 million a year.

Multibranding

While the system plans to open many international units in the years to come, KFC—along with its sister brands—is also pursuing dual-branding opportunities in the United States where it combines two or more of its brands in one location.

"Customers really love the power of our brands and get more variety this way," Novak said. "As an operator, you're taking in 30 percent more than what you'd get otherwise—and that's big. It costs about $100,000 to implement and you pick up $300,000 more in sales. That works big time," Novak said.

Tricon's point man for multibranding and development was Chuck Rawley, who became the chief development officer for U.S. business in 2001 after a stint as KFC president. The title also meant that Rawley was charged with overseeing assets—buying or selling real estate and erecting, remodeling, replacing, leasing, and/or relocating Tricon assets. He also coordinated the "Express" format seen primarily in airports, shopping malls, office buildings, and universities—in smaller buildings with a reduced menu. Rawley also took the point in Tricon's experiment with A&W Restaurants, Inc.

Although Pete Harman (along with Calvin White in Montana) was among the first to experiment with multibranding by combining KFC and A&W in Salt Lake City in September 1998, Rawley was the first to "back into" multibranding between KFC and Taco Bell in a Virginia store as early as 1991.

"That first Virginia location doubled its volume and still is growing today," Rawley said. "It's been remodeled into the new image, but that was the beginning."

Rawley then implemented ten more multibranded locations, mostly in Baltimore, despite antipathy on the part of top management at the time.

"I couldn't figure out anything else that would generate both the consumer awareness and the incremental volume of having two great brands together under one roof with one service counter," he said. "You not only create choice, you leverage the other's brands and marketing programs. Two national marketing programs in the $200-million range, each supporting that concept is pretty powerful. It's turned out to be an extremely successful venture that now is our number-one driver of development."

The Tricon Culture at KFC

"I think the Tricon culture has been a huge plus," Bassi said. "When Tricon was formed, and David started talking about working together, emphasizing the reward-and-recognition culture, a lot of folks at International said, 'That concept might work in America, but it's not going to work in Thailand. Come on.' or 'Gee, I'm not sure that would work.'"

"I said, 'I can't imagine there *isn't* a market in the world where people don't want to be appreciated.'"

"In fact, the culture elements of David's treatise took off internationally *faster* than they did domestically. We were just blown away by how rapidly a lot of this reward-and-recognition stuff spread around the world."

One of Bassi's favorite memories is of an event that occurred at an RGM convention in Thailand. The convention was held outside Bangkok, with a stage amphitheater on the banks of the River Kwai, only a couple of miles from the legendary bridge. On a hot, buggy, steamy night, Bassi waited backstage to give an award. He struck up a conversation with a Thai manager through an interpreter.

"I was killing time and I was really uncomfortable because of the weather," Bassi recalled. "She asked, 'How are you enjoying the evening?'" I said, 'Oh, it's nice. What do you think of this recognition idea?'

"She got this real serious look on her face and said, 'Why would anyone want to work anywhere else?' It was like she put me in my place. I felt guilty even asking the question."

Many of KFC's legacies have become incorporated into the broader Tricon culture. For KFC's employees and franchisees, the most intriguing aspect of the future was to determine how their brand would fit into the overall initiative. As it is with the sister brands, Pizza Hut and Taco Bell, the challenge for KFC would be to continue to differentiate its food offerings in a day when new competitors appear regularly on every street corner.

But the members of the KFC family have long learned to rely on KFC's secret recipe for success, the eleven ingredients that were identified at great cost by their predecessors and have never been more true or more heralded than during the tenure of David Novak. That recipe is the true legacy of Col. Sanders and Pete Harman. And it is that tradition that eventually attracted one of the food-service industry's rising stars to KFC.

A True Believer

KFC cites the handshake between Pete Harman and the Colonel on August 4, 1952, when Harman painted the "Kentucky Fried Chicken" name on his restaurant, as its official founding day, which made August 4, 2002, the fiftieth anniversary of the event. In late 2000, KFC took another page out of Pete Harman's book—naming women to top management roles. The company selected Cheryl Bachelder to become president and chief concept officer.

Bachelder previously served in senior management positions with RJR Nabisco, Gillette, and Procter & Gamble, but it was during her five-year stay at Domino's Pizza LLC that she was tabbed as one of the executives to watch for in the new millennium.

Bachelder said it was the opportunity to work with Novak and his team that lured her away from Domino's. "I knew I was coming to work for a great management team in Tricon and a great brand in KFC, and I was genuinely excited about that," she said.

"The caliber of the people and the culture of KFC is even richer than I ever imagined. It has been rewarding and exciting to see how the Colonel's influence on this company is still alive today—and how the unique contributions and energy of franchisees like Pete Harman make us so successful as a system. Many people have been here 15, 20, 30-plus years, and our system is comprised of seasoned people who absolutely love the restaurant business."

Bachelder also was attracted to KFC because she believed that owner-founded companies have different cultures than standard corporations. It is much easier to create a viable, affirming culture when the values and the culture are personal from the beginnings of a corporation.

"KFC will forever anchor their operations, their food quality, their brand and their values in the Colonel," she said. "I think that sets you apart. It gives you a cultural history. Values in this company go well beyond anything a typical Wall Street firm could create. It's deeper."

The perception remains that the quick-service food industry developed because of the Colonel and McDonald's Ray Kroc. KFC, then, is viewed as one of the founding companies of the industry. According to Bachelder, that perception brings with it both privileges and challenges.

"When you're number one, you have to be careful because that doesn't mean the competition will lie down in a ditch," Bachelder said. "We're in an intensely competitive industry, and you can't rest for a minute or you lose market share. Growth is a constant need and, in that sense, while keeping our equity in the Colonel and our trademarks sacred, we must reinvent ourselves regularly to grow.

"Our challenge right now is that some of our restaurants need to be updated. And we are aggressively going about that—every day we are putting a new store on a site. That's the way you stay in front of your customer—with a great business proposition."

"We are passionately protecting what I call the 'gold standard recipes,'" Bachelder asserted. "In 2000 and 2001, we have gone back, on a very methodical basis, to the Colonel's recipe and benchmark. The technology has changed and there are other things that you adapt to, but the outcome cannot change. The outcome *must* be the great consistent recipes that people have come to expect from us."

Bachelder has a "core belief" about brands—that a company's positioning *must* be to take the basic truths of the brand to the public. Anything else is wasted (where people remember the clever commercial but not the product it is advertising) or counterproductive (where it creates an unreal expectation of the brand that backfires).

> "The one thing that is absolutely unchanged is that the customer knows that the food quality we stood for on day one is what we stand for today. KFC food, made by the recipe, served hot and fresh, is the best fast food in the industry."
>
> —Cheryl Bachelder

"And our truth is the awesome food," Bachelder said, "our truth is that there is nothing like marinated, hand-breaded, freshly made chicken—whether you like chicken strips or chicken on the bone, or popcorn chicken. It has to come out of our truth and our passion. It has to be about our food."

"America has compromised in what they call food," Bachelder said. "And they know it. I think gently reminding people that there *is* an alternative to eating that greasy white-bag food, that you *can* eat it on a plate, that it *can* be hot, that it *can* be freshly prepared, and that it *can* be fast is the way to reignite the customer's passion for KFC. We've got to make sure we're a part of their everyday choices in fast food."

Bachelder has repeatedly saluted the Harman organization for the key role it has played in the food-quality drive—an initiative that's called "Hot and Fresh." Harman spearheaded the renewed effort in their own restaurants and the initiative was expanded to all KFC system restaurants in 2001.

"It's the basic of our business," said Jim Olson, now president of Harman Management, "selling our food fresh. It doesn't sound like any big deal, but with the variety of menus we have and the constraints of time that we have to serve a customer, we need to spend more time emphasizing the freshness element of our business.

"And within a very short period,' he continued, "we have changed a culture that had gotten ingrained in looking at cost management and time management into thinking about quality management. It'll work because we have this 'team together' mentality. Vern Wardle or Jackie Trujillo or myself go out and talk to our people about this. We say, 'This is something we need to change.' And we talk to them as our partners in the business. They want to do what we set out to do. We don't have three hundred stores all saying, 'Well, that's just more work for me. I don't think I want to do it.' People get excited about working together toward accomplishing something for Harman's—not just their own individual store."

An Enduring Legacy

From the Colonel to Tricon, KFC has progressed from a great idea to a global enterprise of unprecedented success. From a handshake to contracts of international scope, from Pete Harman and the Do Drop Inn to Tiananmen Square, the goal has remained constant—*make the customer happy*.

From the Colonel's discovery of the perfect eleventh spice to Pete Harman's serving fried chicken to the first KFC customer, it has always been about pleasing people with *the best damn chicken in the world*.

As KFC enters the new millennium, bolstered by fifty years of accumulated insight, there is little doubt that Colonel Sanders' legacy will continue to guide the entire system.

And it is obvious that Pete Harman's legacy will continue to guide both the Harman Management Group and KFC worldwide.

Together, Pete and the Colonel shared a unique relationship. Father and son, mentor and student.

But it is Pete Harman who today carries the torch of those eleven ingredients for success—and, in doing so, has become the mentor and partner to virtually every KFC leader. His sage advice and support helped KFC through good and bad times.

He became more than KFC's first franchisee.

He became KFC's secret weapon.

As Pete Harman turned eighty-two in 2001, he continued to look toward to the future instead of dwelling on the successes of the past.

"I hope that I'll be remembered as being fair," he said, "particularly in our own company. Arline and I have made a lot of money and we've put a lot of that money into some places that we believed needed it—children's hospitals, public television. Money is only good if you do good with it.

"I think the company under our system will perpetuate itself.

"I haven't had any responsibilities in three or four years. I stick my nose in, but I'm confident the company is in good hands—we've got about four men and women who could run the company right now.

"It isn't like we're going out and changing leadership every few months. The talented people come up from running ten stores to running a group of forty stores. In our system, everybody starts at the bottom. This process produces leaders."

David Novak agrees with Pete that Harman Management will continue to have a positive impact on KFC—and Tricon as well—for years to come.

"You look at the great companies, the great franchise organizations, and they have a definable culture," Novak pointed out. "It's an intangible you can feel. When you go and meet with people in the Harman organization, you can feel it. You can feel it from their actions. Everybody knows they make a difference."

The Harman Culture Defined

➤ We will always remain a privately owned company.

➤ We will provide ownership and/or advancement opportunities for all full-time employees.

➤ We will invest our time and capital to train our existing employees for opportunities for personal development and promotion.

➤ We will do business "Pete's Way"—with the highest level of integrity and humility. At times, we may make mistakes of judgment, never of intent.

➤ We always will maintain our competitive fire to be the best in all we do. We will be the first to take advantage of new opportunities.

➤ We will establish and maintain "win-win" agreements in all our relationships.

➤ We will always keep our "family" social structure, and we will remember that our business success and personal enjoyment come from being interdependent.

➤ We will show compassion to each other and in our communities.

➤ We will ensure that Harman's future leaders will be those individuals whose personal values are consistent with our culture.

"I'm excited about the future," Pete said. "The future means there are more opportunities for more people. The future means there are some people who are going to discover what's really important in life. And that is this—*We tie our success to people, not dollars.*"

For Jackie Trujillo, who has known Pete longer and better than anyone, save Arline, there is a quiet confidence that Pete's philosophies will endure. Why? Because everyone in the organization lives those values.

"Few companies that have had such a dynamic founder carry on after that leader is gone," Trujillo said. "KFC has done it by embracing the Colonel. We're doing it by living Pete's beliefs every day. *We will be one of those companies that thrive. We believe that what we do isn't as important as how we do it.*"

Finally, one last insight from Pete Harman.

The interviewer had a final question for Pete: "What do you think Aunt Carrie would say if she showed up today and looked over what has happened in the past fifty years?"

Pete paused only for a moment and said, "She liked me. She'd still like me."

Harman Management Corporation Operating Values

▶ High expectations of performance
▶ Opportunities for personal and professional growth
▶ High pay for superior personal results/performance
▶ Praise for good personal results/performance
▶ An exemplary reputation
▶ A common culture throughout the organization
▶ Passionate commitment to customer service: Customer is paramount
▶ Openness to and acceptance of change
▶ Increasing profitability
▶ Fun

Appendix

Colonel's Kids

The history of KFC is a history of giving. From the beginning, the Colonel, Pete Harman, and a host of KFC franchisees and employees have made giving to charitable organizations an integral part of who they are.

When earthquakes and fires ravaged the West Coast, Harman Management franchisees responded immediately with generous gifts of food and financial resources. When the horrific events of September 11, 2001 rocked America, KFC was there, feeding exhausted rescue workers, donating blood, and endowing scholarships.

Virtually every KFC franchisee is deeply involved in his or her local community, sponsoring Little League teams, helping at the Salvation Army, giving their fair share to the United Way.

Colonel Sanders' life was marked by his generous, sometimes lavish gifts to innumerable charitable organizations, from churches to hospitals to colleges.

In the year before his death, the Colonel served as national chairman of the March of Dimes. At one time, he was recognized as the largest individual contributor in the world by the Salvation Army. He placed the Salvation Army in a charitable trust to receive annual contributions that have totaled in the millions of dollars.

In fall 2000, KFC launched Colonel's Kids, a program designed to help make high-quality child care available to more families across the United States. With the Colonel's Kids program, KFC's goal is to raise $2 million annually in support of YMCA Child Care. Funds raised by Colonel's Kids will help YMCA Child Care to:

- ▶ Develop programs for extended-hour child care (weekends and evenings)
- ▶ Develop programs for infant/toddler care
- ▶ Fund a toll-free telephone access number to provide the addresses of the closest YMCA Child Care sites

> For more information, please contact a KFC restaurant in your area or call 1-800-874-3273.

About the Author

Robert Darden is the author of twenty-seven books, both fiction and non-fiction on a diversity of subjects ranging from a forthcoming book on Black gospel music to David Koresh and the Branch Davidians. He was the gospel music editor for *Billboard Magazine* for more than a decade and has spent the past fourteen years as editor of The Door. He also teaches creative writing, publishing, and screenplay writing at Baylor University and is a popular speaker at seminars, symposiums, and conferences.

Index